DRUM
USMC
THE
BUGLE
CORPS
COMMANDANTS
OWN
REVOLUTIONARY WAR
FRENCH NAVAL WAR
TRIPOLI
BLADENSBURG
NEW ORLEANS
LAKE CHAMPLAIN
FLORIDA INDIAN WAR
SANTA CLARA
VERA CRUZ
CHAPULTEPEC
BULL RUN
PORT ROYAL

ON PARADE

THE WORLD'S GREAT MILITARY UNITS

Photography and text by Carlos Lorch

Action Editora

ON PARADE

THE WORLD'S GREAT MILITARY UNITS

Designed by André Gonçalves.
Edited by Ross A.Howell Jr.,Anne Douthat and Robert Beadle.

Historical Photos and Paintings-
- Yasukuni Jinja Yushukan Museum.Tokyo
- Imperial War Museum.London (UK,USA,Japan,Canada,Greece chapters)
-National Archives.Washington D.C.
-SIRPA/ECP Armées.France. - Pages 195 - 203
-Photos and Captions Canada Chapter - Kate Armstrong RCMP Ottawa.

Special Thanks:Mr.Jens Jansen,Danish Consulate,Rio. Mr.Piero Ruzzenenti. Mr.Bjorn Nellhede,Swedish Embassy,Brasília. Mr.Amar el Mars,Moroccan Embassy,Brasília. Lt.Col.Adhemar da Costa Machado Filho,Brazilian Army. Commander Rodrigues Pinto,Brazilian Marine Corps. Lt.Col.Giancarlo Rossi,Italian Army. Captain Angelo Palmas,Italian Army. Lt.Pier Luigi Di Rauso,Italian Army. General André Lorant,French Army. Lt.Col.Pierre Fromager,French Army. Captain Verdon,French Army. Captain Pommeret,French Army. Chef D'Escadron Etienne Grech,Garde Republicaine. Col.Ramón Bascur Gaete,Chilean Army. Capt.Alejandro Arancibia Ramirez,Chilean Army. Overstelojtnant Alexander Von Rosen,Swedish Army. Capt.Alejo Arnaiz Marina,Spanish Army. And especially to my loving Wife Monica without whom this would never have been possible.

ISBN 85-85654-03-1

Printed and Bound in Hong Kong
Published by Action Editora Ltda.Av.das Américas 3333/817
Rio de Janeiro,Brazil.CEP 22471-003 Tel/Fax -55-21-325-7229

ACTION EDITORA

This book is dedicated to the memory of Walter Leicester Lorch

CONTENTS

REGIMIENTO GRANADEROS A CABALLO
"GENERAL SAN MARTIN"

ARGENTINA
Army of the Andes
1er Regimiento de Infanteria de Patricios
Regimiento de Granaderos a Caballo General San Martin

Cries of alarm echoed through the streets of Buenos Aires on the cold morning of 25 June 1806. British troops had landed at Quilmes on the southern bank of the River Plate and were poised to attack the city. Four artillery pieces and 1,650 men were swiftly put ashore. The British commander, Gen. William Carr Beresford, wanted no time wasted. Spain had signed an alliance with Napoleon. The Viceroyalty of the Rio de la Plata was now fair game for its British enemy.

The defendants could muster only five hundred badly trained local militia supported by three guns. When the local troops tried to engage the British landing site at Quilmes, the action culminated in their lightning-quick defeat and the loss of artillery to the better-trained British soldiers.

Pushed back to the outskirts of the city, the remaining defenders tried a last-ditch action but were unable to prevent the fall of Buenos Aires. As Viceroy Sobremonte fled to Cordoba with the royal treasure, Spain's major foothold in the South Atlantic was lost to the British army.

No longer defended by the Spanish authorities, resistance was organized by local Criollo gentlemen. Juan Martin de Pueyredón raised six hundred men and marched toward Buenos Aires only to be pushed back outside its limits by the 71st Scottish Regiment. Santiago de Liniers, a French-born officer in the Spanish navy, understood the necessity of organizing veteran troops to face the experienced invaders. Slipping through the British blockade of the river, he led 600 local men along with 370 French sailors from Montevideo to land at Las Conchas on 4 August. In his march toward Buenos Aires, Liniers' force was joined at every small village and hamlet along the way. On 12 August he charged Buenos Aires with 1,500 men, further joined by volunteers from every neighborhood of the city. These "Legions of Urban Voluntary Patricians" formed the main thrust in the violent combat on the streets of Buenos Aires. At the end of the day the British surrendered, boarding their ships to leave the River Plate. Recognizing the weakness shown by the Spanish authorities, the Criollos rejoiced in their "Reconquista" (Reconquest), arming themselves with weapons captured in the struggle as well as with a newly found spirit of independence.

The Patricios push back the British in 1806.

Yet before news of General Beresford's defeat had arrived in London, reinforcements had left the Cape of Good Hope. A 1,900-man corps joined another 4,000-strong force which had left London in seventy ships sponsored by merchants intent on gaining a definitive grip on Spain's South American possessions. On 29 June 1807, more than 8,000 British troops led by Gen. John Whitelocke landed outside Buenos Aires after having taken Colonia and Montevideo earlier that year. The city was able to organize some 8,500 defenders, the majority of which were inexperienced militiamen. The local population began to put up its defenses. After three nights of feverish preparations, they braced for the initial British attack. Fighting wore on throughout the day. At nightfall the British had secured only a few strongholds in the city's outskirts. The center of town remained strongly in the hands of the Patricians. Another attempt the following day proved as bloody and as unsuccessful. The British gained no ground and lost 2,800 men. Losses on the Criollo side were also high, with more than 1,600 dead in the city streets. Whitelocke chose to retreat. After brief formalities and a brisk exchange of prisoners, the fleet left the waters of the River Plate. Jubilant crowds took to the streets of Buenos Aires, while church bells announced the conclusion of what became known as "La Defensa" (the Defense). Although having served the direct interests of Madrid, the Reconquista and Defensa showed the Buenos Aireans that they were able to determine their own affairs, thus paving the way for the overthrow of the Spanish in 1810.

On 29 May 1810, only four days after the Argentine government was established, a government decree gave birth to the first Patrician Infantry Regiment (1er Regimiento de Infanteria de Patricios), thus creating the first official body of the new Argentine army. Spanish troops still threatened the infant nation mainly in the north and west of the Viceroyalty of the Rio de la Plata as well as on the northern bank of the river. Troops were hastily organized and sent into combat, but they failed to liberate those areas.

On 9 March 1812, a man whose military genius was to change the history of the continent landed at the Rio de la Plata, fresh from the Napoleonic Wars in Spain. Lt. Col. José de San Martin arrived in Buenos Aires after resigning from the Spanish army. His mission was to organize a cavalry regiment that incorporated the "maneuvers and principles of the new French cavalry tactics." One week later, he formed the first squadron of the Regimiento de Granaderos a Caballo (Regiment of Horse Grenadiers), a force that would soon become his pride and glory.

Born to Spanish parents at Yapeyú near Paso de los Libres on the Brazilian border in 1778, San Martin traveled to Spain and became a cadet in the Murcia Regiment at age twelve. Three years later he reached the rank of second lieutenant, and at thirty he became a very young lieutenant colonel after distinguishing himself in the fight against Napoleon. When he arrived in Argentina, he immediately set out to instill discipline and esprit de corps among his young troops. San Martin stressed to the government the need to develop a modern and disciplined force, one in which quality was more important than quantity, one that was sharp and proud and ready

San Martin crosses the Andes into Chile.

for battle. Leading by example, he demanded very high standards of military training and instruction. He named each squadron commander personally and asked that each in turn propose his direct second-in-command to establish trust at the earliest stage. Personal hygiene was mandatory, not one stain on the uniform nor a smudge on a button was tolerated. Above all, San Martin created a code of honor for his Granaderos a Caballo that was to be followed unquestioningly.

Slowly San Martin began shaping his Granaderos a Caballo. He designed the regiment's uniform, basing it on that of the Prussian Hussars of the Napoleonic Wars. Every soldier and officer was thus molded personally by San Martin and acquired a strong sense of purpose and self-confidence which was to mark the actions of the Granaderos a Caballo throughout thirteen years of fighting all over the continent.

At dawn on 3 February 1813, San Martin surprised a force of 250 Royalists moving to raid the Convent of San Carlos at San Lorenzo on the banks of the Paraná. His 120 Granaderos leapt from behind the convent buildings and charged in two sixty-man pincers. The Royalists barely had time to close into a defensive position on the outlying plain. In the ensuing melee, the colonel's horse was shot dead from under him. After tumbling to the ground, he was unable to move, his left leg stuck under the dead horse's body. Immediately two Granaderos rushed to the rescue. Private Juan Bautista Baigorria was able to kill a Spaniard who almost succeeded in thrusting his bayonet through San Martin while Sgt. Juan Bautista Cabral freed San Martin but was twice wounded by enemy saber strikes. As the battle was rapidly decided in favor of the Argentine forces, Sergeant Cabral was taken away to die of his wounds. In his agony he pleaded to his companions, "Leave me. We are but a few. I die content. . . . We have beaten the enemy." With forty men dead, fourteen taken prisoner, two guns, forty rifles, and their flag captured, the Royalists retreated toward the river. The first of many charges by the Granaderos a Caballo was a total victory.

To this day, at the imponent headquarters of the Regimiento de Granaderos a Caballo General San Martin in the quiet Buenos Aires neighborhood of Palermo, a solemn ceremony takes place. The oldest of the sergeants stands alone in front of the formed troops at a monument for that act of bravery. On roll call the name "Sgt. Juan Bautista Cabral" is read by the commandant of the regiment. The sergeant takes three steps forward answering with emotion: "He has died for our country but lives on in our hearts. *Viva la Patria, Granaderos*!" The troops cry "*Viva*!" in one voice.

Several battles ensued. Finally the Argentine army was able to take Montevideo, thus denying the River Plate to Spanish ships. The campaign was now ready to proceed into the interior.

By 1815 the revolutionaries were at the foothills of the Andes, constantly pushing the Royalist forces back. Rapidly rising to command the Ejercito de los Andes (Army of the Andes), San Martin soon was able to put his tactics of deception into practice. In 1816 he asked the Pehuenche Indians for permission to cross their territory to attack Royalist positions to the south of the city of Mendoza. Knowing the agreement would fast become known to enemy spies, he attacked his intended objectives to the north instead. Catching the enemy completely unaware, he liberated another important strip of territory in preparation for the great challenge that loomed ahead.

The Army of the Andes, some 4,000 strong, was slowly built up in preparation for the crossing of one of the most formidable natural barriers known to man. The infantry was formed mainly of blacks whose freedom had been purchased by the provincial government. The cavalry was made up of half-breeds, while the officers had been recruited among Spaniards and local Criollos. To the north, the gauchos of Gen. Martin Miguel de Guemes would engage whatever Royalist troops had been left over, thus protecting the main body of the army.

From Mendoza, San Martin made the first step of his campaign in preparation for the crossing. The Guerra de Zapa was a secret war of nerves and cunning in which San Martin shrewdly spread rumors and disinformation to confuse the Spaniards and prepare his tactical position. Knowing he was not yet ready to engage the enemy, he began negotiating a peaceful settlement and the opening of commercial relations with the Spanish commander, General Osorio. Not only did the Spanish authorities take the bait, preparing no defensive positions, but they also sent 1,500 men to reinforce the Viceroyalty of Peru far to the north. Then San Martin leaked out the news that he would invade Chile, forcing the Spanish command to take hasty defensive measures. The spreading of this news, along with several well-placed spies, stirred a popular revolt in Chile that disrupted Spanish preparations.

As the campaign drew near, San Martin spread rumors that he would be invading through the mountain passes of Portillo and El Planchon. He then made certain that a letter addressed to Chilean patriots fell into the hands of the Spanish authorities. In it were the details of his attack through the south. This was followed by rumors that an Argentine fleet had left Buenos Aires, "destination unknown." Throughout the Guerra de Zapa his agents intensified the guerrilla war in Chile. As a result, the defending armies stretched their positions, including their maritime defenses. The main defensive line had 6,000 men covering a 500-mile (800-kilometer) front. The Spanish army did not know where to expect San Martin. He had succeeded in his "Silent War."

On 9 January 1817, San Martin led his army over several passes in the Andes. Some higher than 15,000 feet (4,600 meters) proved extremely treacherous as men and horses, hindered by extremely thin air, negotiated narrow roads among towering precipices. Yet in only twelve days the Ejercito Libertador (the Liberating Army) crossed unopposed into the Chilean plains, a feat never before attempted. On 25 January San Martin's advanced patrols began preparations for the battle of Chacabuco.

On one mission a squadron of one hundred Granaderos under Capt. Mariano Necochea chanced upon a superior force of some three hundred enemy horsemen and four hundred infantry supported by two cannons. After analyzing the terrain, Necochea concluded that the Spanish troops held advantageous positions, but he told his men nonetheless, "We have been sent to the front to fight the enemy, not to look at him," and attempted to draw the enemy out of his position. He made his plan "on the spot," conferring with his men who approved it enthusiastically. A few riflemen were positioned on one of the flanks to cover the rear, and the squadron began a desperate dash from the field they had just reconnoitered. Reading the apparently frantic retreat as an act of cowardice and desperation, the Royalists immediately sent their cavalry into the plains in rapid pursuit. As soon as Necochea sensed that his pursuers were past the protection of their riflemen and artillery, he turned his troops around and charged ferociously in classic Granadero tradition. The enemy froze, stunned, as Necochea and his men tore into them, killing nineteen and capturing four along with more than sixty weapons which the terrified Royalists threw away in their retreat.

As the two armies drew nearer to the hills of Chacabuco, San Martin sent word to his spies to obtain as much intelligence as possible. His irregulars were able to approach the advancing enemy so closely that one of their techniques consisted of counting every man that crossed a particular bridge. At 2 a.m. 12 February 1817, San Martin ordered his troops to move under the light of the moon, denying the advancing Spanish troops time to deploy their artillery. In a pincer movement, the Liberating Army succeeded in dispersing the Royalists, who after fierce resistance began a retreat to the south. They were cut off at the town of Chacabuco and promptly surrendered, leaving 600 dead and 550 taken prisoner. A vast number of supplies, all artillery, and more than 1,000 rifles were captured. Only 11 patriots were killed. Although that great battle had opened the road to Santiago, which was soon conquered, fighting continued throughout Chile. In April 1818, San Martin regrouped, drawing the Spanish forces into a decisive battle that would determine the fate of the campaign.

On 5 April 1818, the Argentine-Chilean army led by San Martin and Chilean liberator Bernard O'Higgins finally defeated the Spanish forces at the Battle of Maipú. The independence of Chile was assured.

By 1820, San Martin had prepared his army for the Campaña del Peru (Peruvian Campaign), boarding his troops on sixteen ships hastily bought or captured by the new Chilean nation. On 7 September, his army landed at Pisco and immediately moved in two columns toward the northern coast and the interior "Sierra." After ten months of slowly pushing the Royalists back, the Liberating Army captured Lima and Callao, thus assuring the independence of Peru. Yet not all resistance had ceased, and fighting continued until December 1824, when the Battles of Junin and Ayacucho clinched the victory for Spanish America. San Martin had met his northern counterpart Simon Bolivar, the liberator of Venezuela, Ecuador, and Colombia, and had left a squadron of his Granaderos a Caballo to assist Bolivar in closing the struggle.

On a hot, dusty afternoon in February 1826 a small group of people on the western outskirts of Buenos Aires gazed in awe as the surviving one hundred Granaderos a Caballo silently rode back into the city after thirteen years of battle. As people gathered around these tired, aged, and scarred men, they were told proudly that "there was no longer an armed Spaniard in all of the continent."

Wars and revolutions followed almost incessantly in Argentine history, the Patricios and Granaderos taking part in all. In

Battle of Maipú. 1818.

1968, left-wing urban terrorists began a bloody campaign of bombings, kidnappings, and shootings to destabilize the government. In January 1970, guerrillas of the Ejercito Revolucionario del Pueblo (People's Revolutionary Army) attacked an army compound at Azul, killing the commander and his wife and abducting a colonel. In 1975, the ERP succeeded in shooting down a plane carrying many members of the army general staff. In the same year, a frigate under construction at the naval shipyards was dynamited and sunk in another daring terrorist raid. In December 1975, some five hundred ERP guerrillas attacked the Monte Chingollo arsenal outside Buenos Aires in what could be considered one of the most daring terrorist strikes of all time. The battle that followed left more than 160 of the attackers dead.

Along with the ERP, another group, the Montoneros, kept the security forces busy. Aside from numerous attacks on army and police targets, they killed the commander of the Argentine police by planting a bomb under his bed. They also succeeded in detonating a bomb in an aircraft parked next to President Videla's plane—fortunately, the president escaped. These daring attacks along with literally thousands of smaller actions prompted the Argentine military to escalate their counter-insurgency measures.

In April 1982, Argentine troops mounted a landing operation and invaded the Malvinas/Falkland and South Georgia islands in the neighboring South Atlantic. After negotiations in 1774, and much bickering and confrontation, the British had left the Malvinas/Falkland islands under Spanish rule. When Argentina declared its independence in 1810, it claimed the islands and took possession of them, an act which was recognized internationally at the time. Yet on 3 January 1833, Capt. James Onslow of the Royal Navy, commanding the frigate *Clio*, expelled the Argentine authorities, imposing British rule. Argentine efforts to regain the islands through diplomacy over a long period failed and on 2 April 1982, war broke out. After the initial invasion, a British task force was mounted and despatched to the South Atlantic. On 21 May the British landed at San Carlos Bay and advanced toward the capital city of Port Stanley. Although defeated on the battlefield, the Argentine army learned from the conflict and immediately set out to restructure itself for the future.

Every day, on the streets of Buenos Aires, guarding the famous Casa Rosada (the Presidential Palace) or the Cabildo (the town hall), are handpicked soldiers of the Granaderos a Caballo and Patricios regiments, a living memory of the struggles of the Argentine people to claim the vast lands from the Andes to the River Plate.

"Of what my Granaderos are capable, only I know for sure. There may be those who equal them, never who surpasses them..." In this manner, General San Martin referred to his special regiment. They became known throughout the continent for their courage and ferocious charges. At the battle of Junin, fought entirely by cavalry units bearing no firearms, Colonel Mariano Necochea, suddenly found himself before a superior number of enemy troops. According to some accounts he turned to his second in command and asked, "How many are there of them? " to which his deputy replied, "Fifty". "And how many of us?" queried Necochea. "Five" came the reply. In traditional Granadero fashion Necochea looked at his men, for a short moment,and said, "So...*al ataque !!!"* Although wounded by 14 punctures and bleeding profusely, Necochea survived to fight on. (Facing) Granadero officers such as this Lieutenant carry, to this day the demeanor introduced by San Martin. Head high to show the national emblem of the smiling sun representing the country's freedom from Spain. Guarding the life and home of Argentina's president, the Granaderos alongside the Patricios, form the Buenos Aires Detachment which brings to life the memories of a glorious struggle for independence.

Formed by civilian volunteers who took to arms to defend Buenos Aires against the British invasions of 1806/7 the Patricios became the first unit of the Argentine army after Independence. (This Page) Their uniform was adapted from civilian fashions of the time in which the civilian militia brought together to defend the city fought. Their badge still bears the old spelling of their city's name. At the Battle of Ayohuma, in 1813,their Spanish opponent was so impressed by their fighting that he stated that: "The Argentine line held its ground with such firmness that it seemed as if they had laid roots on the soil they were defending..." The Patricios fought in every major struggle of the Argentine nation. It is therefore fitting that the blue and white of the Argentine flag, originated from the color of the uniforms used by those brave men who first defended Buenos Aires.

JAPAN
Land of the Divine Wind
302nd Military Police Company

In the year 1274 the great Mongol leader Kublai Khan had reached the Korean seashore in his conquering sweep eastward. The islands of Japan lay in his path toward the rising sun. Undaunted by the barrier of the ocean, Khan assembled a Mongol-Korean fleet and launched an invasion force. After conquering a few small outlying islands, they landed in full force on northern Kyushu and soon established a bridgehead, pushing the Japanese defenders back. Miraculously as the Mongol army prepared to spread inland, a powerful storm swept in from the east, wreaking havoc on a large part of the fleet. Japanese reinforcements also descended upon the landing sites, forcing Khan to pull back to Korea.

Seven years later, the undaunted Khan carefully prepared yet a stronger invasion force, comprising some 4,500 junks and 150,000 troops. From moorings in Korea and northern China the powerful force set sail on another foray to subdue Japan. They again landed in northern Kyushu but met fierce resistance from Japanese land and sea forces for two arduous months. Suddenly another violent storm descended upon the straits, obliterating the invading fleet. Stranded with their backs to the sea, the Mongol troops were harried by the advancing Japanese. Only a few thousand survived to return to Korea. The people of Japan thanked their gods for sending them the *kamikaze* (divine winds) that saved their sacred land.

The Japanese are historically tireless warriors. The art and science of warfare have always been central to Japanese culture, although these values only became evident to the western world in the present century. From its inception, the samurai code of *Bushido* (the way of the warrior) dictated combat ethics and procedures, emphasizing honor and loyalty, the temporary nature of one's existence, and the triviality of death. Combat followed traditional rules and rituals, and strategy was scientifically conceived.

Before a battle, samurai warriors would eat the three lucky dishes, dried *awabi* (shellfish), *kombu* (seaweed), and chestnuts, with a ceremonial toast of *saki*. Each samurai warrior would then proclaim to the enemy his name, lineage, and deeds of war. The Bushido dictated that only worthy opponents could engage in combat. The samurai were armed with their *daisho*, a pair of curved blade swords consisting of the longer *katana* and the shorter *wakizashi*. These were used with the cutting edge fitted upwards so that a deadly blow could be delivered directly from the scabbard. Lance, bow and arrow, and later the harquebus were also used in the early wars of the samurai.

Massive troop movements would take place on the battlefield using standard battle formations conceived for every possible situation. Thus the attacking *hoshi* (arrowhead) charge could be countered by the *saku* (keyhole) defensive move or even the *koyaku* (yoke) lineup, a flexible defense also efficient against the *kakuyoku* (crane's wing) move of encirclement.

For special operations behind enemy lines and assassinations, as well as for the rescue of important hostages, the Japanese warlords maintained the *Ninja* warriors. Clad in black and proficient in special martial techniques, these stealthy infiltrators still capture the imagination as invincible warriors of the night.

The samurai chief directed his troops from a commanding vantage point over the battlefield. He would sit inside a *maku* (a curtained structure) and direct his forces through messengers and flags. After a successful battle, the victorious warlord would remain inside his maku for the viewing of the heads. The taking of an enemy's head was proof of a job well done. The heads were washed, the hair was combed, and they were mounted on a wooden board and held in place by a spike. One by one, the samurai would march past the chief displaying the heads of important enemies. The warlord would examine each head and offer his comment, which was generally praise for the samurai and respect for his opponent.

Samurai warrior.

Sino-Japanese battle scene, 1846.

The samurai period lasted until 1870 when the *mikado* deposed the shogunate and assumed full power. A new army was formed and now anyone could become samurai, a distinction

Japanese forces, Java oilfields. 1941.

previously reserved for the aristocracy. Trained by German instructors, the new army was soon able to prove itself. It won a decisive victory against a massive Chinese army in the Sino-Japanese War of 1894, adding vast amounts of territory to the home islands.

On 8 February 1904, after diplomatic negotiations over Manchuria and Korea had failed, Japanese troops made a surprise attack on Russia's Far East naval base at Port Arthur. After an initial charge in which 15,000 men were killed, Gen. Maresuki Nogi lay siege to the Russian positions with heavy artillery bombardments. After almost a year, Port Arthur finally capitulated after grueling trench combat. The naval battle for the straits of Tsushima clinched the war for Japan in a stunning and unexpected victory. For the first time, an Asiatic force had defeated a strong European army. Suddenly, Japan was recognized as a world power.

After the war, the Japanese army was stationed in Korea and Manchuria. From 1932 to 1945, they clashed with the Chinese and Russians, gaining important military experience. On 7 December 1941, the preemptive Japanese attack on Pearl Harbor thrust the U.S. into World War II. Throughout the war, 8,000,000 men were mobilized, seeing action on a wide front that extended from the Aleutians to the doorstep of Australia and from Hawaii to the Indian border. The Japanese had introduced samurai ethics into modern war with devastating results. In Malaya, Gen. Tomoyuki Yamashita's outnumbered Twenty-fifth Army sped down the peninsula in three months of brilliant jungle fighting, finally taking Singapore in February 1942. This was the most humiliating defeat in British military history. More than 80,000 men lay down their arms in surrender. Only 9,824 Japanese casualties were recorded. In Bataan and Corregidor in the Philippines, more than 90,000 U.S. troops surrendered to the Japanese. In contrast, Japanese troops employing the Bushido philosophy consistently held their ground. In tiny atolls, in China, Burma, New Guinea, and over the vast Pacific, Japanese soldiers, sailors, and kamikaze airmen valiantly gave their lives for the emperor. At Iwo Jima in February 1945, out of a total garrison of 23,000 troops, only 216 came out alive. On Okinawa, out of 130,000 defenders, 110,000 were killed. Staunch, valorous foes to the mighty American and British forces, the Japanese fought to the bitter end, earning the unenviable distinction of being the only nation bombed with atomic weapons.

Out of the ashes rose modern Japan. The Japanese were allowed a token defense force by the occupying Allies, and so emerged the Ground Self Defense Forces, the GSDF.

Armed and equipped with U.S. materials, the Japanese army has been revamped completely. At first glance, Japan's elite guard unit, the Dai 302 Hoan Chutai (302nd Military Police Company) resembles a ceremonial unit of the U.S. Army. The uniform, headgear, and even the traditional American manner of parading the flag in the center of ranks show a strong U.S. influence. The serious demeanor, the unflinching loyalty to those in command and to the civilian leaders of the GSDF, and the rigid, almost mechanical perfection on parade ground attest to the fact that the Japanese will always be first-class soldiers. Formed in 1954, the Dai 302 Hoan Chutai is responsible for all ceremonial duties in the Japanese army. Perfectly clad in their green winter uniforms or their elegant white summer dress, with shining new M-1 Garand 7.62-mm rifles, they are engaged in honor guard, VIP guard, and traffic control duties nearly every day. Their spartan Tokyo barracks, adorned with nothing more than a wooden plaque stating the unit's name, are home to three platoons numbering roughly one hundred men who rotate between guard duty and regular military training in Japan's small but very professional army.

Japan's modern army is limited to the defense of the home islands and at first glance resembles little of the samurai warriors from the past. Yet should the need arise they would surely fight with the same spirit as that inscribed on the battle banner of warlord Katsuyori Shingen: "Fast as the wind, firm as the mountain, free from sound as the forest, fierce as the fire!"

 The Japanese Army takes Christmas Island, 1941.

横浜倉庫

立入禁止

Camp Shibaura is home for Japan's elite Dai 302 Hoan Chutai. Squeezed between the sprawling capital and Tokyo Bay the unassuming compound is typical of Ground Self Defense Force bases. Primarily a peacetime defense force, the GSDF has adopted the cherry blossom (Right) as its symbol. Discipline is high in the Japanese army and drill is practiced to perfection. Uniform and equipment such as the ubiquitous M-1 Garand 7.62-mm rifles (Top) are similar to those used by the U.S. Army, although the elegant summer uniform (Facing) is unique.

SWEDEN
The Blue Dragoons
The Royal Lifeguard Dragoons

Although Sweden has been at peace for more than 150 years, from 800 to A.D. 1000 ferocious hordes of Nordic Vikings wreaked havoc throughout Europe. Owing their names to the *wicks*, small hidden coastal inlets where they lived protected from high winds and seas, the hardy Wikings, or Vikings as they are now known, were originally a poor people who traded in hides and slaves.

These tough, able-bodied Norsemen saw opportunity in the constant quarreling between the peoples of the continent. Sailing in their sturdy, wide-bottomed longships and landing on remote coastlines, they mounted violent raids against coastal villages, ransacking, raping, and hijacking in the process. Viking warriors were fearless, believing that when they died they would go to *Valhalla*. In the Norse heaven, fallen warriors were immediately healed so that they could rejoin battle.

The terror they spread with their actions made them bolder, and soon Viking parties were sailing up the mouths of Europe's rivers, including the Thames and the Seine, capturing horses to add to those they brought on their ships and attacking cities miles inland. They conquered vast territories and began charging *danegeld*, a toll that guaranteed passage through strategic sea routes as well as a temporary interruption of Viking attacks. Danish and Norwegian Vikings sailed westward to conquer Normandy, large parts of England and Scotland, reaching as far as the coasts of North America. The Swedish Vikings, who called themselves "Rus" or "Ros," concentrated their exploits in the east, giving rise to the name "Russia."

Both raiders and traders, the Swedish Vikings soon spread southward with the Russian rivers. Under their great leader Oleg they seized the city of Kiev. In 907, they sailed a large fleet down the Dnieper River and when it ended, they portaged their ships overland and reached the Black and Caspian seas. Without much opposition, they invaded Constantinople, where they extracted a highly profitable trading agreement with the Byzantine Empire. Impressed by their martial abilities, many of the Byzantine emperors employed the Rus, whom they called Varangians, as personal bodyguards, a tribute to their superior fighting skills and discipline.

For many years, scholars doubted that the Vikings had reached so far south. However, discovery of ancient Swedish inscriptions on one of two famous stone lions provided the missing proof of the Vikings' existence in the area. The lions were captured by the Venetians at Constantinople and now adorn San Marco Square in Venice.

As the Vikings began to create their own kingdoms, they ceased rampaging and slowly relinquished the ascendancy that had spread terror to all of Europe.

After several years of union with Denmark and Norway, Sweden finally went on its separate path in 1523 under King Gustavus I, or Gustavus Vasa. After defeating the Danes and turning the country toward the Lutheran faith, the king created the foundations of the modern Swedish state, including a well-equipped and efficient army.

Swept into a series of small conflicts in the Baltic, the Swedish army soon joined Protestants in the Thirty Years War of 1618-48 against the powerful Catholic forces of the Hapsburgs and their Spanish allies. The Swedish army that joined the fray in 1630 was blessed by the inspired leadership of King Gustavus II Adolphus, a brilliant military genius considered by many to be the "Father of Modern War."

Ascending the throne in 1611, Gustavus II Adolphus, or Gustav Adolf, spent his entire reign in war. Against the Danes and the Russians, he showed great expertise in military skills, applying classical theories learned from the great campaigns of Hannibal, Alexander, Caesar, and other strategists of antiquity. He adapted these theories to his own needs and introduced modern concepts that placed him among the most brilliant military leaders of his time.

Instead of counting upon foreign mercenaries, as was the custom, the king created a national conscript force recruited from the wealthiest citizens of his reign, men who were well fed and had reason to fight. The troops were well paid and a system of pensions and land grants was created for veterans to instill corps morale and to settle troops close to the people for whom they were fighting.

Gustav Adolf reduced the size of his regiments from three thousand men to a thousand, thus increasing speed and mobility in the battlefield. He invented the squadron and the brigade, formed to mold firepower to movement. He also made sure his soldiers carried lighter weapons and redesigned heavier models in his quest for flexibility. The bulky wheel-lock muskets lost several pounds and could be fired without the cumbersome supporting bipods. Cartridges containing powder and shot were distributed to ease reloading. The pike was shortened and artillery was mounted on wheels so that it could be moved around, actually accompanying the infantry. His revolutionary light cannon could be drawn by one horse or three men.

Gustav's army concentrated even more fire and shock than the famed Spanish Tercios and the battalions of Maurice of Nassau from the Netherlands. Instead of countermarching after firing a volley, the Swedish squadrons employed a simpler tactic where two ranks fired simultaneously in salvos of great effect. The ineffective fashion of the day was to trot up to the closed enemy ranks to fire pistols and retreat to load. His cavalry, wearing a minimum of body armor, were trained to press home their attacks with pistol and sword, employing speed and shock with flanking maneuvers.

At Breitenfeld, north of Leipzig, the battle between Sweden and their Saxon allies and Count Tilly's Catholic League army on 18 September 1631 demonstrated the effectiveness of Gustav's tactics. At the River Lech, he maneuvered his artillery to cover a river crossing and completely destroyed an enemy caught unaware. His decisive victory furthered his reputation as the "Lion of the North" and saved the Protestant cause.

Swedish victories in Gustavus II Adolphus' time were a combination of tactics, good military administration, and high morale. The Warrior King was equally preoccupied with the front line as he was with his rear guard. High-quality standardized training for all troops created a sense of professionalism and self-esteem. The troops were led by caring and professional officers.

The king himself was a brilliant leader, as evidenced by his public dispute with Colonel Seaton, a distinguished officer in his army. During a public display of his troops, the king, annoyed with the colonel for a minor reason, struck him before the troops. After the field day was over, Colonel Seaton demanded his discharge from the army, which was signed immediately by a silent king. When he was informed that the colonel was leaving the kingdom to offer his

Swedish Dragoon in early uniform.

services to Denmark, the king immediately set off on horseback to the Danish border. Intercepting Seaton on a vast plain, the king rode up to him, instructed him to dismount, and offered him a duel on equal terms. Recovering from the initial shock, Seaton dismounted and falling to his knee thanked the king for granting him the opportunity as an equal, but said he could not risk "that my sword should do any mischief to so brave and gracious a prince!" Instead, he asked for the honor to return and serve the king until his death. Gustavus II Adolphus then raised him from the ground and embraced him, settling the dispute. The two men rode back to Stockholm, arriving as best of friends before an astonished court.

Gustavus II Adolphus died at age thirty-eight during the Swedish victory at Lutzen. Sweden's army, however, lived on. For the next eighty years it was virtually unbeaten throughout Europe.

In 1658 Sweden fought the First Northern War against Poland, taking Warsaw, then moving into Lithuania. King Charles X led the Swedish army in a daring move. To counter a surprise Danish attack on its rear guard, the army crossed the frozen waters of the Belts between the Danish islands with troops, cavalry, artillery, and supply wagons. It was considered an impossible deed, and the king was strongly cautioned against the move. Yet, Charles stood his ground, and his army was soon threatening Copenhagen.

His son, Charles XI, who finally conquered what is today the southern counties of Sweden from Denmark, reorganized Gustav Adolf's concept of the army and among other things standardized the uniform. Charles XII ,who ruled Sweden from 1697 onwards was another warrior king. He engaged the Danes, Poles, and Russians, and nearly reached the gates of Moscow before he was turned back by the harsh Russian winter. Decimated by the cold, his troops numbered only 21,000 men from the original 80,000. They besieged the city of Poltava on 13 July 1709 only to meet 77,000 Russian troops led by Peter the Great and supported by more than one hundred guns. The Swedes, however, accepted the fight. Even when all was lost, they charged more than 40,000 Russian troops head on. At the end of the day, Charles XII led his surviving men into Turkish territory and safety. Swedish power was virtually eliminated after almost one hundred years of military brilliance.

It was at Poltava that Gustav Adolf Creutz, the Commanding officer of the Life Regiment of Horse was captured by the Russians. Before surrendering his weapons, he was able to conceal a gold chalice used by the Swedes to celebrate mass before battle. For eighteen years, Creutz managed to keep the sacred object safe. After years of searching the Life Regiment assumed it had been lost in battle and had a second chalice made. Finally repatriated, Gustav Adolf Creutz had the honor to return the venerated gold chalice to his regiment where it remains today, an object of great reverence, stored in the luxurious guards' barracks in Stockholm.

During the Napoleonic Wars, Sweden participated in an alliance with Russia, Prussia, and Austria against the French emperor. After a few small conflicts in the early 1800s, Sweden fought her last war in 1815 against Denmark and Norway. Although neutral in both world wars, the Swedish army has remained extremely well trained and equipped, and Swedish troops have been employed in every United Nations operation since the Korean War.

The Kunglig Livgardets Dragoner K 1 or the Royal Life Guards Dragoons - the Horse Guards , is together with the Svea Life Guard - the Foot Guard, Sweden's Royal Household troops. Composed of one battalion of Horse Guards (K 1) and one battalion of Foot Guards, the Life Guards are responsible for Guard duties in Stockholm's Royal Palace. Formed originally in 1523 the Swedish Guards are probably the oldest regiment in the world. Based at the splendid central Stockholm guards' barracks, the guards double as a military police unit, trained to act as special forces if needed. In their royal blue uniforms, inspired by German fashions of the 1800s, complete with a shiny white metal *picklehaube* (spike-bonnet) and Swedish-made 6.5-mm 1894-model Mauser carbine, they are known nationwide.

Mounting bay Swedish horses, the Mounted Royal Lifeguard Dragoons create quite an impression as they ride down the streets of Stockholm toward the royal palace. They are generally led by a mounted band, which is famous throughout Sweden. In fact, competition to join the mounted band of the guard is so fierce that several hundred volunteers apply during each recruiting season. Particularly impressive are the two 33-pound (15-kilogram) kettledrums mounted on large English horses, which were donated by Queen Elizabeth II. All horses in the regiment, in typical Swedish pragmatism, are loaned from a civilian foundation of breeders,private owners,and the public, thus freeing the army from high ceremonial expenses. Since it is an honor to have one's horse participate in the royal guard, the animals are magnificent.

The guards are billeted in the wonderful gold-crown-topped barracks in Stockholm, a large, spotlessly clean compound where the cavalry elements are housed. Upon arriving at the stables and cavalry drill ground one notices the incredible number of dogs lingering amidst horses and privates. Following an age-old Swedish cavalry tradition, each officer has his own dog. A recent order by the Swedish high command banning dogs was met with such resistance that the order was quietly dropped and the tradition continued peacefully.

Recently, the tone of the guards' uniform was also changed from a dull Prussian blue-gray to a dazzling royal blue that lights the streets of Stockholm with color. Recent studies by historians of the Swedish army conducted on microscopic fibers of museum-piece uniforms discovered that the original blue, faded and worn with time, had been adopted from generation to generation of Swedish guards. The Swedish army has once again adopted the original shade of blue, which probably hails from King Gustav II Adolphus' times.

Elegant defenders of a wonderful nation, the Royal Lifeguard Dragoons are the living descendants of one of Europe's most formidable armies.

- (Facing Page) The Royal Lifeguard Dragoons are Sweden's handpicked royal guards in service of King Carl XVI Gustaf. Members of the band wear red epaulletes on their shoulders. (This Page Right) The guard duty officer carries a small metal breastplate reminiscent of the cuirasses of yesteryear. Charles XI once ordered a bullet shot at every cuirass to ensure that his soldiers were well protected. Therefore, all cuirasses in the Swedish army had a bullet dent. (Top Right) The king receives the royal salute at the palace. (Above) Horse guards' mounted drummer.

TUNNELBANA

Two kettledrummers ride large English horses. Flag bearers ride white stallions. Other than these, all mounts are bay Swedish breeds.Before the Swedish Army was uniformed the field sign for a Swedish soldier during battle was a piece of straw attached to the men's hats.Tradition remains in a small roundel of straw around the cap badge in the modern uniforms of the regiment.

THE VATICAN
Keepers of the Holy See
The Swiss Guard

Embedded in the center of Rome, the Vatican City is a fascinating miniature country seating the head of the Roman Catholic church and its ruling bodies. Drenched in tradition, the 109-acre (44-hectare) compound composing the imponent Basilica of Saint Peter's and various administrative buildings attracts the faithful from all corners of the globe. Unfortunately, through the years it has also attracted the enemies of the church, in the form of both invading armies and internal conspirators. For almost five hundred years the Holy See has been defended by an elite corps of Swiss guards. Recruited from Switzerland's Catholic cantons, the Swiss guards are the living descendants of the great warriors that dominated European warfare for more than two hundred years.

The original Swiss, known as Helvetii or Helvetic Celts, were last subdued by the powerful Roman Legions from the south. Thereafter, they resisted many invasions that tore through Europe and remained free until the thirteenth century when their independence was threatened by the ambitious Austrian Hapsburgs. In 1291, three small villages on the shores of Lake Lucerne, known as the Waldstätte or the forest cantons, joined forces against the Austrian threat. The "Everlasting League," formed by the three village states of Uri, Schwyz, and Unterwalden, became the basis of the *Schweizerische Eidgenossenschaft* (the Swiss Confederation) which was to number thirteen members by the 1500s. Their fighting spirit, tactics, and military organization would have an enormous impact on European warfare. For centuries, the mounted knight had been the undisputed master of the European battlefield. Swiss innovations once again brought the foot soldier to the forefront of military thinking.

Shock was the major weapon of the Swiss halberdiers and pikemen. Armed mainly with twenty-foot (six-meter) pikes, the Swiss formations completely neutralized the charges of mounted knights in armor. Each of the four ranks held their pikes differently. The first would kneel with the long pike held low, while the second stooped with the pike's rear butt pressed under the back foot. The third rank held the pike at waist height, while the fourth held it at the shoulder, using it in a jabbing action from top to bottom. The Swiss would raise their pikes and halberds against enemy arrows, forming an impenetrable forest of wooden shafts.

Inside the thick body of pikemen were the halberdiers. Their weapons were a mixture of an axe and a javelin on a six-foot (1.8-meter) shaft, excellent for both cutting and spearing. Other warriors were armed with heavy two-handed swords and the Lucerne hammers (heavy spiked clubs). Some Swiss wore light armor and helmets, but the majority fought in light civilian attire which gave them incredible speed and mobility. Crossbowmen and later musketeers were used as skirmishers before the columns of pikemen, which were generally subdivided in three groups: a vanguard, the main body, and a reserve unit.

The Swiss armies were extremely organized. Conscription was determined by the joint or local council of elders. Depending upon the gravity of the campaign, larger or smaller armies could rapidly be mobilized. There were basically three categories of Swiss soldiers. The Auszug was the elite corps, formed mainly by the younger unmarried men between the ages of eighteen and thirty. The Landwehr was composed of fit family men who were prepared to leave their homes and families if necessary. The Landsturm was the bulk of the male population, used only in a general emergency such as a complete national revolt. Well-oiled communication and mobilization systems guaranteed a fast call to arms.

At Morgarten against the invading Austrians in 1315, Swiss tactics carried the day. A carefully planned ambush was sprung at a chosen mountain pass. While a forward group attacked the head of the Austrian column, blocked by fallen trees, rocks, and earthen debris, throngs of Swiss warriors swept from the slopes at both sides, completely massacring the helpless Hapsburg knights and foot soldiers. The Austrian army was ten times the size of the attacking Swiss force.

At Sempach in 1386 the Swiss, using only halberds, came across the Austrian pike. At a certain standstill in the encounter, Swiss ferocity finally carried through. A certain Swiss soldier known as Arnold Von Winkelried is reported to have thrown his body at the wall of enemy pikes, taking out several of their points and snapping the shafts with the weight of his body. The Swiss then poured into the momentary opening swinging their halberds above their heads and chopping through the Austrian pikemen.

Several victories such as Náfels, the Appenzell Wars, Arbedo, Grandson, Morat, Nancy, and many others soon had all of Europe not only fearing the burly Swiss but also hiring some of their number as mercenaries. Charles VIII of France formed the "Hundred Swiss" in 1496, the first full Swiss unit outside Switzerland.

In 1503 while ascending to the throne, Pope Julius II created a special unit for the protection of the pope and the Apostolic palaces. On 22 January 1506 a company of 150 men recruited from the canton of Zurich entered Rome led by Gaspard de Silen. Eventually their numbers were increased and they began fighting for the church throughout Europe. They fought with such bravery at Ravenna in 1512 that Pope Julius II granted them the title of "defenders of the freedom of the church." In 1517 they faced the forces of Francesco da Rovere and his Spanish allies and in 1521 defeated the duchies of Parma and Piacenza.

On 6 May 1527 Spanish and German mercenaries under Constable Bourbon sacked Rome and the Apostolic palaces. Starving and unpaid, the invaders were particularly brutal and committed numerous atrocities throughout the city. Palaces and churches were sacked, nuns were raped and auctioned, while the citizens of Rome were killed and thrown into the Tiber River. Soon the plague would engulf Rome. A steadfast last stand by the Swiss Guard at the Church of Saint Peter's allowed Pope Clement VII enough time to escape. While the Swiss Guard fought to the last man, the pope was led through the underground secret passage of the Borgo to the nearby fortified palace of Sant'Angelo.

Today, a beautiful engraving in white marble adorns the wall of the guards' courtyard in the Vatican. Every year on the sixth of May, the new guards take the oath of the corps in a wonderful ceremony in honor of those few brave Swiss of 1527.

In France, Swiss mercenary troops continued in vogue. Louis XIII's Swiss Guards were among the most experienced troops in the empire. At the Battle of Rossbach in the Seven Years War,

Frederick the Great was vastly impressed by the Swiss troops. The battle had already been lost for the French but the Swiss Guards refused to surrender. An intrigued Prussian king inquired of one of his aides, "What are those red brick walls which my artillery cannot breach?" On being told their identity, the king remained silent, then solemnly raised his hat to their resolution.

During the French Revolution, the Swiss Guards were completely destroyed while defending the Tuileries from the enraged populace. Swiss regiments were also present with Napoleon at Waterloo. After that great battle, the Council of Vienna forbade Switzerland to further export mercenaries, other than those guarding the pope. In Rome, they continued their service faithfully. In 1914, Pope Pius X fixed their number at one hundred soldiers and six officers, including the commandant with the rank of colonel and the chaplain.

Although in peace for more than four hundred years, Switzerland still possesses one of the best-equipped and organized people's armies in the world, employing the philosophy of their forefathers of the 1500s.

Today the Swiss Guards are responsible for the custody of the entrances to the Apostolic palaces as well as for the cobblestone line that divides the Vatican from Rome. They also guard the pope's residence at Castel Gandolfo and provide the pontiff's escort on all state functions. They guard the basilica and the papal antechamber. When the pope is not in residence, the Swiss Guard serves the cardinal chamberlain, who becomes responsible for maintenance of order in the Vatican.

The selection process is very thorough, as only the best and most reliable volunteers are accepted to the guard. The Vatican's recruiting brochure, printed in Switzerland's four languages, asks for Swiss citizenship, excellent health, a minimum height of 68.5 inches (1.74 meters), and membership in the Roman Catholic religion. Young hopefuls must be bachelors and must produce a maturity diploma or a professional certificate. Finally, they must hold an "irreproachable reputation," usually conferred by a knowing member of their local clergy.

Once selected, they are sworn in at a ceremony held at San Damaso court every sixth of May. As high-ranking members of the church, officers in the Swiss and Italian armies, and the proud families of the new recruits watch in awe, the entire Swiss Guard marches into the afternoon sun clad in their vibrant *cinquecento* uniforms, cuirasses and all. After forming up and presenting halberds, each man marches to the center of the patio where he clutches the guards' standard and pronounces the oath of unquestioning defense of the pope and the church. The entire ceremony transpires as if directly out of the Renaissance itself, a deeply touching moment carried out privately behind the imposing walls of the Vatican.

The Swiss Guards use a dazzling Renaissance ceremonial uniform of blue, yellow, and red stripes, with white collar and gloves, a steel Morion helmet with crest, and a cuirass which is used solely on the sixth of May. Although some have said that the uniform was designed by Michelangelo and Raphael, the two great masters had no hand in the design, although the latter did create the ample sixteenth century *manche bouffante*, flared sleeves which were adopted by the guard. In fact, five guards appear in his famous *Messe de Bolsene* fresco.

Officers use the same burgundy uniform sported at the entrance of Pope Clement VIII in Ferrara on 8 May 1598. Their helmets are of white steel with a burgundy plume. The commandant sports a white plume. The men also wear a fatigue uniform consisting of dark blue jerkin, short blue trousers, black stockings, and a black drooping Raphael hat.

Weapons include the traditional halberds and swords, although officers carry a saber. In papal processions some non-commissioned officers carry the heavy two-handed broadsword with undulating blade, symbolizing the loyalty of the Catholic cantons.

The flag is carried by a NCO clad in black and burgundy with a helmet sporting a white plume. The beautiful silk banner of the Swiss Guard is divided into four fields by a white cross. The coats of arms of Pope Julius II and of the reigning pontiff appear in two of the fields. The other two fields bear the guards' colors, one yellow and the other red and blue. The center of the cross carries the coat of arms of the serving commandant.

On a quiet spring Wednesday in 1981 Pope John Paul II made his weekly appearance to meet the faithful on St. Peter's Square. Suddenly gunfire tore apart the tranquil buzz of the morning. Terror swept through the crowd. The pope had been shot at close range. A young Turkish hoodlum, Mehmet Ali Agca, was wrestled to the ground and captured. To the immense relief of the world, the pope survived, after being rushed to hospital and undergoing an operation. Subsequent investigations turned up possible links with the Bulgarian Secret Service and a vast underworld organization linked to that country.

The attempt on the pontiff would have enormous effect on the Swiss Guard. Until then mostly a ceremonial and light crowd control unit, the guards began extensive training in a series of new security measures and techniques. Judo became mandatory, as well as training with small arms. Guardsmen were seen more often with two-way radios, and the use of mace, paralyzing gas, discretely concealed in the uniform was also initiated. Responsible for the pope's security while abroad, selected Swiss guardsmen became expert bodyguards, knowledgeable in every form of modern security procedure.

Although dressed in colorful Renaissance dress, the Swiss Guards retain a tough and serious demeanor. They are quite aware of the potential dangers faced by the modern-day church. Yet not all is drill and vigilance in the life of a Swiss guardsman. Fully integrated among the one thousand inhabitants of the city-state (the guards even have their own soccer team), they are housed in comfortable apartments and carry their daily duties from the guards barracks located just off Santa Ana Gate. The barracks include the geranium-lined Guards Courtyard, a small museum, and the Armory, where spotless uniforms, cuirasses, swords, and halberds line the walls and overhead racks. Offices and a small gymnasium are also part of the guards' domain.

On duty the Swiss Guards evoke images of bygone days when they were prepared to fight off invading armies for the glory of the Holy Church. To watch the sole Swiss Guard sentry standing, halberd in hand, at the head of the stairway to the Vatican's Bronze Gate, while the warm spring's setting sun casts him in a golden hue, is to relive a distant past in a sweet fleeting moment.

ADITO ALLA BIBLIOTECA ED AL MVSEO

(This Page) Descendants of the great Swiss soldiers who once dominated European warfare, the Swiss Guards at the Vatican are responsible for the direct protection of the pope and the holy palaces. (Top) Preparing to march into St. Peter's Square, the guards form up in the guards' patio in front of the marble monument for the dead in the 1527 defense of Rome. (Right) Officers wear an elegant burgundy uniform. (Facing) Guarding St. Peter's on Easter Sunday.

-(Facing) With three fingers for the Father, Son, and Holy Spirit, new Swiss Guards swear allegiance to the church on the touching 6 May ceremony at San Damaso Court. Note the two-handed ceremonial swords with undulating blade. (This page) Drummers and trumpeters hail the guard in a manner reminiscent of the brilliant days of the Renaissance. Modern-day dangers however, force the guards to discretely carry radios and cans of nerve gas under their cinquecento uniforms. The commandant of the guard is the only officer to wear a white plume on his Morion helmet.

ARRAS

GREAT BRITAIN
For Queen and Country
The Household Division
Yeomen Warders of the Tower of London
The Gurkhas

If any one people were to be singled out to embody military spirit it would have to be the British. No one else has the same respect and zeal for drill and training. The elegance and precision of British military ceremonies are famous worldwide and are an integral part of the islands' beloved pageantry. Tradition is the building block of British institutions, and in the army it is a way of life. British military history is vast, permeated with acts of bravery and heroism. Many times over the world has watched in awe as the resolute little islands bore the brunt of powerful enemies, often with extraordinary results.

Archaeological studies indicate that warfare has been waged in the British Isles since about 3000 BC. The invading Roman legions were unable to beat Britain's valorous ancestors, the Celts, prompting them to build the famous protective Hadrian's Wall to keep the warriors away in Scotland and Wales. The British also trace their military background to the invading Normans, who decisively defeated the Saxons at Hastings in 1066.

During the Middle Ages, British tactics and techniques ensured the growing tradition of warfare. Catapults bombarded fortified cities and castles, launching projectiles such as incendiary material, heavy rocks, and even dead and rotting horses in an early attempt at chemical warfare. Captured spies and hostages were also catapulted into the ramparts as a means of intimidation. The English longbow wreaked havoc on mounted knights. British victories at Agincourt, Crecy, and Poitiers during the Hundred Years War with France proved the superiority of Britain's archers on the battlefield.

Britain's tremendous success in the military field is the product of long-ingrained fighting spirit, bravado, and outright toughness. Frederick the Great of Prussia, one of the world's most brilliant warriors, once asked Sir Robert Sutton at a review of his tall grenadiers whether he thought an equal number of Englishmen could beat them. Sir Robert replied, "Sir, I would not venture to assert that, but I know that half the number would try."

Throughout the years, British bravery and unquestioning discipline under fire have produced gallant charges. During the Crimean War, at 6 P.M. on 25 October 1854, the light brigade charged into the flaming mouths of Russian batteries. The action prompted an amazed French general Bosquet to murmur, *"C'est magnifique mais ce n'est pas la guerre!"* ("It's magnificent but it is not war!") On the terrifying first of July in 1916, after eight days of intensive bombardments to weaken German defenses, a huge British offensive was unleashed at the Somme to relieve German pressure on Verdun. As wave after wave of British infantry advanced through the muddied landscape of water-filled shell holes, German machine gunners mowed down the advancing surges. The massacre was horrendous, but the pace of the attack never faltered. More than 40,000 men fell in the first three hours of the attack. By the end of the five-month offensive 450,000 men had died.

British soldiers also excelled defensively, mastering the precise science of concentrated and well-aimed firepower. At Dettingen during the War of the Austrian Succession, the Royal Scots Fusiliers stood poised while the French charged. Their commander bellowed, *"Dinna fire till ye see the white o' their een,"* while the French moved ever closer. The results were devastating; the British broke the French impetus with massive volleys. The order they received became a battle cry of defensive firepower for years to come.

At Waterloo, Britain's guards formed tightly knit defensive squares and beat away several charges by Napoleon's elite troops. At Balaclava 650 men, of which one hundred were invalids, braced to repel the entire Russian cavalry with the sobering order from Sir Colin Campbell: "Men, remember there is no retreat from here. You must die where you stand." The troops responded with a cheer. The defenders lay in wait, as the massive waves of Russian cavalry thundered up the rolling slopes. Suddenly, the "Thin Red Line" rose as if emerging from the earth itself, two deep with rifles aimed and

Grenadier Guards, Crimean War, 1850s.

at the ready, every man with his target. The surprised Russians hesitated long enough to take the first deadly volley of musket fire that swept hundreds to the ground. Regaining their composure, the Russian cavalry began a charge exactly when the second volley hit them in full. The Russians faltered and the Redcoats surged forward to engage the horsemen hand-to-hand. "Ninety-third! Ninety-third!" bellowed Sir Colin, "Damn all that eagerness!" With perfect discipline, the line steadied and fired a third volley at the enemy. The remaining Russians fled in desperation toward the main body of their cavalry while the British troops burst into cheers.

Eccentricity is another marvelous British trait. Colonel Owen Williams, who commanded the Blues (the Royal Horse Guards) in the late 1800s, is a prime example. Among other antics, he would choose a route from Windsor to London that led him directly to the banks of the Thames. Undaunted, he would ride

Yeomen Warders of the Tower of London, 1800s.

straight into the river in full uniform and swim his horse across, emerging soaked but elegantly poised with a large cigar still burning in his mouth.

Perhaps the most eccentric of all was "Mad" Jack Churchill of the commandos. He epitomized British bravado during World War II by leading his men into battle carrying a longbow, a broad-hilted claymore, and a bagpipe which he played at every conceivable moment, to the horror of his troops and the enemy. Without a drop of Scottish blood in his veins, Jack Churchill nevertheless honored the Highland war spirit as if he were descended from generations of ferocious Scots. Once he was asked why he went to war with a sword on his belt, to which he indignantly replied, "Any gentleman without a sword is improperly dressed."

Mad Jack Churchill's greatest moment came in the small Sicilian town of Pigoletti. Ordered to take the hilltop village from a German force that outnumbered his men, he devised a cunning nighttime charge. Spread out across the vast valley, his men advanced up thickly wooded slopes. Yelling "Commando! Commando!" at the top of their voices, they gave the impression that they were a much larger force, allowing each man to know where his colleagues were in the darkness and instilling terror in the defending Germans.

Upon reaching the town, Mad Jack had outpaced his troops and found himself alone. Seeing two German sentries standing under an open door frame, he stealthily moved around them. Suddenly from out of the darkness the terrified sentries saw a bizarre and horrible apparition: Mad Jack Churchill was waving his sword like a man possessed and spitting out a flurry of incomprehensible German. Only two words were understood, *"Hande höch!"* with which the two men complied immediately. Finally catching up with their commander, a few commandos were given the men to guard, and Mad Jack disappeared into the darkness after another target. This time he came upon a mortar pit and to his utter disapproval found the crew asleep around the weapon. Unceremoniously he kicked each man in his backside. As they awoke they were greeted by the sword-toting demon rudely screaming, *"Hande höch!"* In this manner, Mad Jack captured more than thirty men before the night was over — without firing a single shot.

Britain has fought on every continent and on each of the seven seas. Her battle honors are great. Each generation of British soldier seeks to add glory to the long list of British battlefields around the globe: Blenheim, Dettingen, Quebec, Ramillies, Assaye, Brandywine, Salamanca, Waterloo, Inkerman, Delhi, Omdurman, Amiens, Gallipoli, the Somme, Ypres, Dunkirk, Crete, El Alamein, Normandy, Arnhem, Burma, Malaya, Goose Green. With each bloody conflict the British army has increased its tremendous military experience in the science of waging war.

The Guards

No military ceremonial in the world is as well known as the changing of the guard at Buckingham Palace, performed by the Household Division in London. More than five million attend annually, making it one of England's most famous sights. The Household Division comprises two regiments of Household Cavalry, the Lifeguards and the "Blues and Royals," and five regiments of foot guards, the Grenadier, Coldstream, Scots, Irish, and Welsh guards. Their motto, set in the Household badge inside a garter star, is *"Septem Juncta in Uno,"* Latin for "Seven Joined in One."

Since the time of Charles II, when all but the Irish and Welsh guards were raised, the guards have been the personal troops of the sovereign, guarding the royal family in both war and peace. The sovereign is the colonel in chief of all seven regiments and places great importance in participating yearly in all events, wearing in turn the uniform of each regiment.

The history of the Household Division begins with the English Civil War of 1642-48 when King Charles I faced a rebellion in Ireland. Parliament refused to send English troops, deciding instead to raise ten Scottish regiments to be sent across the sea. The king intended to lead the expedition personally and therefore raised a personal bodyguard, commanded by the Marquis of Argyll. The Scots Guards trace their ancestry to this regiment.

Defeated by Oliver Cromwell, Charles I was executed but left his son to fight on. Charles Stuart brought an army from Scotland but was defeated at the Battle of Worcester and almost captured by Cromwell's "Roundheads." While being led into the Boscobel Oak by Colonel William Carless, he was able to escape to Flandres. The episode is commemorated today by the Household Cavalry, who

Lawrence of Arabia.

wear an oak leaf and acorn on their helmets and on the tips of their aiguillettes.

With Cromwell's death in 1658, Prince Charles, exiled in Bruges, decided to form a troop of horse guards from among the Royalists who had followed him to exile. Originally eighty strong, this regiment would number six hundred upon Charles' restoration in 1660 and eventually became the Royal Lifeguards. The Royal Regiment of Guards, also formed in Bruges by the king, would become the First Regiment of Foot Guards upon restoration, and later the Grenadier Guards.

In England, General George Monck's regiment was to play a significant role in the restoration of Prince Charles to the English throne. Oliver Cromwell had raised the regiment for then-Colonel Monck as part of the new model army. Conscious of a prevalent atmosphere of unrest, Monck led his troops from their quarters in the small Berkshire village of Coldstream on the English/Scottish border and marched upon London. Without bloodshed he broke the army's domination of government and elected a new Parliament. One of the first resolutions passed by the house was the reinstatement of the king. A Roundhead general had thus contributed to the king's restoration to the throne. At Canterbury on the way to London, King Charles II met with General Monck and bestowed upon him the Order of the Garter, which remains the symbol of his regiment. After his death his troops became popularly known as the Coldstreamers and in 1817 were officially designated the Coldstream Guards.

The horrors of the civil war over, England and the army could again trace a common path. To avoid further rupture, the king created a standing army, the base of the modern British army. One of the new regiments created was the Royal Regiment of Horse, later the Royal Horse Guards. The king also raised a regiment to defend the new trading post of Tangier in northern Morocco. The port was dowry presented to England for his wife, the Portuguese heiress Catherine of Bragança. The regiment, aptly named Tangier Horse, served with distinction against the Moors for twenty-two years. Upon its return to England, it was renamed the Royal Dragoons. With England back to normal, the guards protected the sovereign in peace and war. They were however the only disciplined body of men left in London at the time. Their duties therefore included police work, the quelling of riots, and firefighting.

War was soon declared against the Dutch, and both the First Regiment of Foot Guards and the Coldstream Guards saw their first actions — surprisingly at sea. Several officers even commanded men-of-war and General Monck won several naval engagements. He would often give orders in inappropriate land terms to "wheel right" or to "charge!" In 1664 the Coldstream Guards captured New Amsterdam, the capital of Dutch North American possessions, and promptly renamed it New York in honor of the king's brother, the Duke of York.

Two years later the Scottish regiment was officially granted the title of the Scottish Regiment of Foot Guards, from which the Scots Guards were brought up.

In 1678 the foot guard regiments each received a grenadier company armed with hatchets and grenades. To allow for easy maneuvering of the flintlock and for good arm movement when tossing grenades, these companies were given a sort of bishop's miter, adorned with decorations and mottoes in Latin, rather than the original headgear. In 1768, bearskin was added to this hat and the decorations combined in a metal front.

British soldiers on the march in northwestern France, July 1916. Note wounded German prisoner.

When Charles II died in 1685, he was succeeded by his brother James whose short rule was marked by toil and hardship. James was toppled in 1688 by the Dutch Protestant Prince William of Orange, who was crowned King William III. Guard duties in London were carried out for a period by his own Dutch lifeguards, mounting grays and wearing blue tunics. Due to that elite troop known as the Dutch Blues, the Royal Horse Guards, also sporting blue, became known as the Oxford Blues (they were commanded by Aubrey de Verre, earl of Oxford). Nearly three hundred years later, in 1969, the Oxford Blues would be amalgamated with the Royal Dragoons (the Royals), forming today's "Blues and Royals."

In the 1700s the guards again saw action in North America during the Revolutionary War. Once again they took New York and, though the British fought well, they eventually lost their American colonies. In that war, light companies were formed to respond to the lightning guerrilla strikes performed by the Americans. The static, en block, parade-ground style of warfare was modified for the first time in more than one hundred years.

The Napoleonic Wars lasted twenty-two years, with the British army constantly fighting in Flanders, Egypt, Portugal, and Spain. The Coldstream Guards carry the badge of a sphinx and the word "Egypt" on their colors to commemorate their daring operations on North African soil.

On the Iberian Peninsula, the guards began a tradition that would set them apart from the rest of the British army. During the famous retreat from Coruña, 15,000 British troops, ragged and demoralized, pushed away from the front to regroup and recuperate. Like zombies the men dragged their tired bodies through the hot, hilly terrain. Meanwhile, out in the distance, the survivors from the two battalions of the First Guards strode by in marching order with drums beating, the drum major twirling his baton, and the men marching in step. That simple display of military prowess rebuilt morale which would eventually help sweep Napoleon from the peninsula.

A few years later, the guards again saw a day of glory when they met Napoleon on the fields of Waterloo. At the Chateau de Hougoumont, the guards beat back five stubborn attacks and successfully held that important position while inflicting more than 8,000 casualties on the enemy against 540 of their own. At the decisive moment of the battle, when the British squares had already contained the French cavalry, only 1,000 yards (915 meters) separated an advancing force of 3,000 grenadiers and chasseurs of the unbeaten French Imperial Guard from some 1,000 infantrymen of the First Guards lying in ambush behind the crest of a small hill. Behind them on horseback, the Duke of Wellington could see the French advancing. His men could only tremble in anticipation while listening to the tramping of feet and shouts of *"Vive l'empereur!"*

At the last possible moment, Wellington gave the order. As the guards rose to their feet, the two elite troops saw each other for the first time. Almost immediately the guards fired a volley, then another. When the French recovered from their initial shock and began a haphazard charge, another thundering blast further thinned their ranks. The First Guards charged on bayonet, pushing the Imperial Guards back. Throughout the battlefield the rumor spread like brushfire *"La garde recule!"* Seizing the moment, Wellington

A British soldier teases a Turkish sniper at Gallipoli.

waved his hat, and with a resounding cheer the whole British army swept forward.

Upon returning home, the First Guards were granted the title Grenadier Guards for having beaten the formidable French grenadiers of the Imperial Guards. They also adopted the bearskin hat, which was common only to the grenadier companies in the guards regiments. In 1832 all regiments adopted the bearskin.

The Household Cavalry also saw distinguished action at Waterloo. The Royals captured the eagle standards of the French 45th and 105th infantry regiments. The Blues and Royals commemorate that feat to this day by wearing the badge of an eagle on their left arms.

Corporal John Shaw of the Lifeguards, a famous boxer before being drawn into the army, used his strength to his advantage. On just one charge he cut down eleven enemy soldiers, decapitating one and parting another's skull in a swift strike. He later found himself fighting dismounted and alone against ten Frenchmen. He downed five before his sword broke but continued fighting, first with the hilt of his sword and then with his helmet until he was finally cut down by a bullet from an enemy rifle.

The Scots in their kilts, advancing with pipes wailing and screaming as they charged, filled the air with a terrifying sound that earned them the nickname "Ladies from Hell." Waterloo is perhaps the single most revered day in Britain's amazing military history.

The second half of the nineteenth century saw the guards fighting in Crimea, Egypt, and South Africa. The Household Cavalry Brigade made history at el Kassassin when they relieved a besieged British garrison in the famous Moonlight Charge. They also formed a camelry corps mounted on dromedaries, which accompanied a force down the Nile in Thomas Cook's tourist steamers in order to relieve the garrison of Khartoum.

To commemorate the bravery shown by Irishmen against the Boers in the South African veld, Queen Victoria formed an Irish regiment of foot guards, the Irish Guards. While they were commemorating their first St. Patrick's day as a regiment, a delivery of many boxes arrived containing a personal gift from Queen Alexandra. Inside the boxes were sprigs of shamrock which the guards immediately placed in their caps. A tradition was born and has never been broken since. The shamrock, grown in Ireland by the O'Keefe family at Rosscarbery near Cork, is now given by the Queen Mother to the Irish Guards on St. Patrick's Day, even when the regiment is posted overseas.

A tale is told of an occasion in the 1920s when the regiment, posted in Constantinople, received its shamrock brown and withered. A quartermaster promptly addressed the disappointed commanding officer, saying he would take care of the problem. As promised, on St. Patrick's Day the troops were presented with fresh green shamrock. When asked how he performed such a miracle, the quartermaster answered, "Well, Sir, I gave it what you and I like best . . . a bit of Irish whiskey."

The guards fought valiantly through the slaughter of World War I. During the retreat from Mons on 30 August 1914, the Fourth Guards Brigade passed another British force resting by the roadside. Without formal orders, the men shouldered arms and marched past, heads upright while a few harmonicas played one of their regimental marches. In 1915, King George V formed the Welsh Guards who were performing guard duties immediately afterward.

At Dunkirk in the opening days of WWII the Third Battalion Grenadier Guards marched toward the beaches with arms sloped just like their forebears at Coruña 130 years earlier. According to Field Marshall Lord Alexander of the Irish Guards, they arrived in Britain with their trousers pressed.

During WWII, the guards saw action on every British front. In the desert they formed the elite Long Range Desert Group, a unique special reconnaissance force of volunteers from the Scots and Coldstream guards. To them was added the Special Air Service (SAS) formed by a maverick Scots Guardsman, Second Lieutenant David Stirling. These units mounted daring raids behind the lines, striking at German airfields and Afrika Korps supply lines. The SAS breached the wire fence at Sidi Haneish Airfield and drove their eighteen jeeps in a mechanized cavalry charge in V-formation, obliterating all German aircraft in sight. After that incredible display of British bravado, the raiders disappeared into the night.

On one occasion near Anzio in Italy, the battalion headquarters group of the Irish Guards was surrounded and taken prisoner by a larger German force. As they were being marched off, the guards turned on their captors with any weapon they could lay their hands on, spades, belts, seized rifles, even a large petrol tin was tossed. They succeeded in killing twenty Germans and taking another nine prisoner.

At Cassino, the Welsh Guards sent out radio messages in their native tongue to disguise their identity from the Germans. Soon their positions were showered with German propaganda leaflets urging them to surrender . . . in Urdu. They had been mistaken for Indians.

After the landings in Normandy, the Welsh Guards also led the lightning spearhead into Belgium and the low countries. They liberated Brussels on 3 September 1944. To this day, the Mannekin Pis, Brussels' famous statue of the mischievous toddler, includes in his wardrobe a uniform of the Welsh Guards which he proudly dons every year on Liberation Day.

After WWII, the guards continued to serve in every conflict involving the British army. From Palestine to Malaya, Borneo, Aden, Northern Ireland, the Falklands/Malvinas, and the Persian Gulf, there has always been a guards regiment present wherever Britain wages war.

Although at first all the foot guards seem the same in red tunics, bearskin caps, and SA-80 rifles, each regiment possesses in its particular uniform details that identify the men from their brothers in arms. The plumes placed on the bearskins according to the regiment's position in line are singular. The Grenadier Guards sport a white plume worn on the left side following a tradition started by the grenadier companies in all regiments. The Coldstream Guards, nicknamed the Kiddies, adopted a red plume on the right in 1832. They formed on the left flank and the plumes facing inward were clearly visible on parade and in battle. The Scots Guards marching in between carried no plume. Later, with the forming of the Irish Guards (blue feathers or bristle according to rank, worn on the right) and Welsh Guards (white-green-white plume on the left), the line-up was formed by all five regiments.

The particular guards regiments are identifiable by the spacing of their uniform buttons as well. The grenadiers carry them spaced singly, the Coldstreamers in pairs, the Scots in threes, the Irish in fours, and the Welsh in fives. The collar and shoulder badges also denote regiment. While the grenadier carries a "grenade fired proper" on the collar and the royal cipher on the shoulder, the Coldstream wears a garter star and a rose respectively. The Scots Guard is recognized by a star of the Order of the Thistle on the collar and a thistle on the shoulder. The Irish carries a shamrock and a star of the Order of St. Patrick, while the Welsh sports the leek in both badges.

The officers' uniforms differ slightly, mainly with gold or silver embroidery on tunic and badges, wider stripes on the trousers, a crimson or gold sash rather than a white belt for the grenadiers, and larger bearskin caps.

Although each regiment possesses a corps of drums and a drum major, all clad in a uniform embroidered with fleurs-de-lys from Stuart times, the Scots and Irish guards in addition have a corps of pipers and a pipe major. The Scots pipers wear a plaid and kilt in

Scottish troops scout open ground at the Somme. 1918

British troops charge the Afrika Korps at El Alamein

royal Stuart tartan and an ostrich feather bonnet with a blue and red hackle. The Irish pipers sport their traditional green and orange uniform.

The Irish Guards, also known as the Micks, are the only regiment in the Household Division officially allowed a regimental mascot. In their case, an Irish wolfhound leads their parades. The Welsh Guards have so many sons, brothers, nephews, and cousins in the regiment that the repetition of names has become a problem. The regiment has therefore adopted a system, common in most Welsh regiments, where the two last digits of a soldier's service number precede his name.

The Household Cavalry Division, formed by the Lifeguards (popularly nicknamed the Tins) and the Blues and Royals, mount black Irish chargers, each measuring sixteen hands. The trumpeters mount grays and the drummers ride heavier horses, generally with skewbald or piebald markings. The horses' manes are brushed to the left by the Lifeguards and to the right by the Blues and Royals. They have mounted the guard at Whitehall for more than three hundred years, both as mounted sentries and dismounted guards, controlling the official entrance to Buckingham Palace. The Household Cavalry daily mounts the sovereign's Lifeguard and provides all necessary escorts. When the queen is in residence a "long guard" is formed, comprising one officer, fifteen other ranks, and a standard. When she is away from London, a "short guard" of two NCOs and ten troopers mounts the Lifeguard.

The Household Cavalry's dress uniforms have remained unaltered since 1865 and comprise red tunics with blue and gold facings for the Lifeguards and blue tunics with red and gold facings for the Blues and Royals. Both wear the white metal, Prussian-style, spiked Albert helmet with civil war, lobster-style fasteners and a garter badge flanked by St. George and the Dragon. The difference lies in the horsehair plume that falls from the spike; while the Blues and Royals wear a red plume, the Lifeguards sport a white plume shaped like an onion on top. Trumpeters in both regiments wear a red plume. The chin strap is also worn differently, as the Lifeguards balance theirs on the point of the chin, rather than under the chin as do the Blues and Royals. The shiny, white metal cuirasses, long, highly polished jackboots, a white pouch belt, gauntlets, white breeches, and aiguillettes drooping from the left shoulder are common for warrant officers and NCOs in both regiments as well.

The musicians of each regiment, who are trained to perform mounted, do not wear cuirasses. On state occasions they appear in a gold-embroidered state dress with a blue velvet jockey's cap. The farriers are armed with oversized axes from more than two hundred years ago, used to deliver the coup de grace to horses wounded beyond hope on the battlefield.

Due to a royal ordinance made by Charles II after a series of attempts on his life, the colonel of the Lifeguard was given the direct personal protection of the king as his utmost responsibility. The colonels of the household regiments have to this day maintained the appointment of Gold Stick in Waiting and Silver Stick in Waiting (held as a reserve to the Gold Stick), responsible for the close protection of the sovereign. The colonels of each of the two regiments, which have included men such as the Duke of Wellington and the Earl of Mountbatten, are on duty on alternate months and take precedence over all other officers on state occasions. Perhaps the most visible and world-famous of these occasions is the tradition of trooping the color. Derived from the ancient custom of parading the flags or standards in front of the ranks, the process insured that each man would be able to recognize his own unit's flag, which was used as a rallying point in the heat of battle. The colors, always carried by an ensign, have become an object of reverence and symbol of the regiment's feats of bravery. Today the ceremony is carried out on the queen's official birthday in June.

Precise, elegant, disciplined, and carrying in their colors centuries of bravery, the guards of the Household Division are perhaps the regiment that best embodies the qualities of the British soldier.

Yeomen Warders of the Tower of London

Another bastion of British history is the Tower of London and the small force of Yeomen Warders assigned to keep watch over it. The men have been assigned to the fortress and its prisoners since 1078 when the foundations were laid by the Norman king William the Conqueror. The forty or so Yeomen Warders today serve mainly as guides and in administrative functions, yet with the same sense of devotion and purpose as in the past. The corps was formed in 1509-10 by King Henry VIII who, despite leaving the tower to reside elsewhere, kept in place a detachment of twelve yeomen of the bodyguard formed by his father Henry VII in 1485.

Edward Seymour, duke of Sommerset, imprisoned in the tower in 1549, was the man responsible for the present status and livery of the Yeomen Warders. Deeply impressed by their effectiveness and cheerful spirits, he vowed to grant them any wish they pleased if and when he was released from his cell. A year later he was pardoned and freed. True to his promise he accepted their wish of being allowed to wear the same uniform as the yeomen of the king's bodyguard. Subsequently, there has been much confusion about these two separate units. The Yeomen Warders of the Tower of London wear the same uniform as the yeomen of the queen's bodyguard of the Yeomen of the Guard, with the exception of a gold embroidered sash draped over the left shoulder of the bodyguards. Once used to carry a harquebus, the sash is part of the Yeomen of the Guard's uniform only.

Formed after the Battle of Bosworth in 1485 by King Henry VII, the Yeomen of the Guard parade as a special unit of bodyguards to the sovereign on state occasions. The Yeomen Warders, on the other

Lt. Colonel David Stirling greets a mostly Guards composed SAS patrol in the western desert.

hand, have always served guarding the Tower of London. Dressed in daily dark blue undress uniforms from Victorian times, the modern day Yeomen Warders are selected for the forty-two posts at the tower from retired warrant officers and color sergeants from the army, Royal Air Force, and Royal Marines. They guide visitors through the tower grounds, guard the crown jewels kept in a specially designed vault at the tower, and maintain the ancient tradition of the Ceremony of the Keys. This ancient tradition of locking up the Tower of London every night probably began in Norman times when the White Tower dominated all of London and its approaches. It has been carried out every night without fail for more than seven hundred years.

Over the years, the tower eventually became the royal residence, the state mint, and a royal prison. Much of the nation's gold, royal records, and regalia were kept there and a real concern existed over possible forays by the surrounding populace to free prisoners or steal the crown jewels. Every night at dusk, the Chief Yeoman Warder joined by an armed escort locked and secured all doors. This done, the keys were given to the Tower Governor who kept them for the night. In 1826 the Duke of Wellington, then Governor of the Tower, changed the time of the ceremony to 10 P.M. to allow all soldiers to be safely inside the tower before the gates were locked.

Every night at exactly seven minutes to 10, the Chief Warder marches down from the byward tower clad in the traditional scarlet watch coat and Tudor bonnet, carrying in one hand a lantern lit by a piece of candle and the queen's keys in the other. After picking up his escort he proceeds to each gate, locking it in the process. As the keys pass the sentry boxes manned by the guards of the Household Division, the sentries present arms. After being challenged at the Bloody Tower Archway by a zealous sentry, the Chief Warder meets the night guard, salutes the sovereign, and then takes the keys to the house of the resident governor for the night.

The ceremony of the keys was continued throughout the Blitz in WWII, even when a German bomb landed on the tower so close to the escort that the men were thrown to the ground. As if nothing had happened, they picked themselves up, reformed, and completed the ceremony.

The Chief Yeoman Warder carries as a symbol of his office a ceremonial mace with a silver model of the White Tower at the tip. Other Yeomen Warders carry special appointments. The Yeoman Gaoler, responsible for overlooking the prisoners as well as their guards, carries to this day a ceremonial axe, rather than an executioner's axe, which was carried in front of the prisoners as they were marched to trial. On the way to court, the axe was carried with its blade pointing away from the prisoner. If he or she were found guilty, the blade would be carried pointing toward the prisoner as a subtle way of announcing the verdict.

The Yeoman Raven Master cares for the large black ravens that make the Tower of London their home. His appointment dates to the reign of Charles II when the Royal Astronomer working on the tower complained to the king that the birds were getting in the way of his observations. The sovereign ordered the removal of the ravens only to be reminded of the ancient Norman legend predicting that the White Tower would crumble and with it the throne of England if the ravens ever left the tower. The cautious king decided to leave just a limited number of the birds, a custom that is maintained with great zeal.

On special occasions, such as Easter, Christmas, Whitsun, a coronation ceremony, a royal salute, an inspection of the bodyguard, the installation of the Constable of the Tower, or when the child of a Yeoman Warder is married in the Chapel Royal of St. Peter and Vincula within the tower, the Yeomen Warders wear their splendid state dress. These marvelous and costly uniforms are made "by appointment to the queen" by the Saville Row house of Compton Sons and Webb. They are composed of scarlet and gold doublet; breeches and stockings of the same color with red, white, and blue rosettes fastened just below the knee; black buckled Monck shoes (named after Exon Roger Monck); and the black velvet Tudor bonnet with red, white, and blue ribbons around the crown.

Introduced by Henry VIII in place of the green and white Tudor uniform, the scarlet doublets carry on front and back the marvelously embroidered badge. The badge consists of the monarch's initial and the letter R for the Latin word rex or regina, the crown, and the floral decorations of a rose for England, a thistle for Scotland, a shamrock for Ireland, and a Tudor crown for Wales. The Yeoman Warder carries a sword and a partisan, a pike-like tapered spear measuring seven feet (two meters) with a blade and wings at the base. The partisan is used both as a weapon and as a measuring stick to adjust ranks and level fire. To this day, the slow walk and the traditional position of "stand at ease," with hands joined in front over the shaft of the partisan and legs casually apart, continue a tradition of elegance and confidence among the keepers of the tower.

British bicycle troops land in normandy during D-DAY.

British tommies fighting in the ruins of Monte Cassino.

To many, the Yeomen Warders are known as "Beefeaters," although they themselves dislike this name intensely. According to some accounts the nickname originated in the reign of Henry VIII when he raised their pay to four shillings a day, a hearty sum at the time for such delicate guard duties. The pay generated protest by many who labeled the yeomen Beefeaters for earning enough to include beef in their diet.

At one point, posts at the tower could be purchased and turned into quite a profitable trade if a Yeoman Warder retired. If he died in service, however, the money was collected by the Constable of the Tower. The traditional toast is still heard today when a new warder is installed at the Ceremony of the Punch Bowl, "Yeoman Warder, may you never die a Yeoman Warder," a life of duty and tradition in what is without a doubt one of the oldest military corps in existence.

Gurkhas

The country of Nepal is hidden amid the towering, snow-covered Himalayan peaks and the impregnable valleys and forests of its lowlands. The people are a mixture of Mongolians, Tibetans, and Aryans who have found solace in the rough roof of the world. Living in flimsy mud and stone houses precariously perched over ridges and precipices of the Himalayan foothills, several Nepalese tribes have maintained their ethnic distinction through the ages. Life in Nepal is often one of deprivation and poverty. Contact with the outside world is fairly recent and has been slow to reach most outlying areas. Few maps are available and local units of measurement, such as the *rumale-kosh* (handkerchief mile), have been invented by the mountain tribes. This measurement takes into account the time a wet handkerchief hanging from a walking stick takes to dry.

Some fifty miles (eighty kilometers) from Katmandu, the country's capital, lies the ancient principality of Goorkha from which a warrior caste of indomitable soldiers hail. The Gurkhas, as they came to be called, are small, black-haired, almond-eyed villagers of Mongolian stock. Despite the toughness of their daily lives, in which a walk to a water hole may involve strenuous climbs over steep, high-altitude trails, they have not lost their optimism, strength of character, and tribal pride. Young children, often dressed in nothing more than rags, clamber up steep hills every day after herds of sheep, working lungs and legs to athletic perfection in the thin mountain air. The word Gurkha means "protector of cows," and through fierce

Gurkha troops march through Rangoon, World War II.

fighting and deeds of honor, they have become true princes of the battlefield.

In 1768, Prithwi Narain Shah from Goorkha completed the conquest of Nepal. The Valley of Katmandu was the only known territory at the time; the rest of the country was known as "the hills." Expanding rapidly, the new Gurkha Empire in 1812 stretched from the Kashmir border to Bhutan and soon clashed with another growing force pushing up from the subcontinent to the south, the British East India Company.

In 1814 the first of two bloody campaigns broke out between the warrior nations. Fighting was fierce, and each side gained tremendous admiration for the other. At the British siege of the Gurkha fort of Kalunga, an incident demonstrated the wonderful innocence of the Gurkha warrior. In the midst of an artillery bombardment, a lone Gurkha appeared from the fort and walked briskly toward the British lines waving his hands. Rejoicing for the first surrender, the British officers ordered a cease-fire and welcomed the lone Gurkha enemy into their lines. His jaw was shattered, yet after having the British medics patch him up, he immediately asked permission to return to the fort and resume the fight.

A clear indication that respect was mutual occurred when Lt. Frederick Young, leading a small patrol of native sepoys, suddenly encountered a group of Nepalese soldiers. His own troops fled for their lives. Young refused to run and was soon captured by a group of amused Gurkhas. When asked why he had not fled with his troops, he answered that he had not come so far to run from the enemy. The Gurkhas approved of his attitude saying, "We could well serve under men like you."

Finally at the decisive British victory at Malaun, Gurkha general Amar Singh was allowed upon surrendering to leave his fort bearing his weapons, colors, two artillery pieces, and all his personal property, a rare honor in that brutal corner of the world. The two nations signed the Treaty of Segauli of 1815 in which, in exchange for a brigade of Gurkhas, the British offered Nepal peace and territorial sovereignty. It was the beginning of a lasting friendship. Soon, Gurkha soldiers were seeing service with the East India Company, popularly known as the "John Company." This led to the lasting nickname, "Johnny Gurkha." The first Gurkha battle honors came at the six-week siege of Bhutopore, a combined British-Gurkha operation in 1825-26. It was at that battle that the Gurkhas were heard to say, "English troops are almost as good as us."

In 1857, Indian *agents provocateurs* spread the rumor that the gun grease used in British rifle cartridges for the new Enfield rifles employed by Indian sepoys was in fact made of pork and cow fat, prohibited by the Moslem and Hindu faiths respectively. Since the soldier had to tear at the cartridge's cardboard shell with his teeth, he was being tricked, said the rumor, into the loss of his honor before his religion. A bloody mutiny ensued in which Delhi was taken by the rebels and throughout India whites were massacred. Loyal Indian troops were immediately given special "ungreased" cartridges in order to defend British positions. On the eve of the mutiny, however, the Gurkhas demanded that they be given the same cartridges as those used by the British soldiers. From the north, Nepalese troops led by Maharajah Jangabahadur Rana, who had made the prohibited "voyage over the black water" to meet Queen Victoria, crossed the border to assist their British allies.

The Gurkha name was soon feared and respected throughout the subcontinent. On India's northwest frontier, British troops fought several wars against ferocious mountain tribes. The Pathans were particularly feared due to their custom of taking no prisoners or wounded alive and of mutilating and castrating their enemies for sheer pleasure. The Mahsud, one of the most brutal Pathan tribes, used to say however that they feared only the Prophet and a Gurkha with his *kukri*, a curved-blade knife. The Pathans, when lined up against Gurkha trenches, would shout at them, "We don't want you! Where are the red-turbanned ones [the Sikhs] and the white men?"

When World War I erupted, more than 200,000 Gurkhas volunteered to serve the British army and saw action in every theater of war in which the British army took part. More than 20,000 Gurkha casualties in France, Flanders, Mesopotamia, Persia, Egypt, Suez, Gallipoli, Palestine, Salonika, and on the Russo-Turkish border proved their loyalty and fighting spirit. Thrown into the cauldron from the primitive ways of Nepal, many Gurkha soldiers boarded troopships unaware that the world was round. Having never seen the ocean, many thought that the troopships had legs underneath the water. Yet their innocence, pride, and sense of duty added to their reputation in what was perhaps history's most brutal war. The battle cry of *"Ayo Gurkhali!"* ("Here come the Gurkhas!") became known and feared worldwide. A small troop of Gurkhas even volunteered for action disguised as Bedouins on camelback with Lawrence of Arabia.

In WWII, forty battalions of Gurkhas fought in Syria, the Western Desert, North Africa, Italy, Greece, Malaya, Singapore, Burma, Imphal, and Rangoon against Germans, Italians, and Japanese. In the Far Eastern jungles they excelled, laying grounds for their eventual actions in Malaya and Borneo. Although originally from the Himalayan highlands, the Gurkhas were skilled in the jungle. They possessed patience, perfect eyesight, high alertness, and an ability to track and read terrain found only in the best of jungle hunters. Their kukri also seemed designed for use in the jungle. In Britain's postwar jungle confrontations, the Gurkhas have been in great part responsible for resounding success.

Originally recruited only from Gurkha tribes, the Gurkha regiments now take in youngsters from throughout Nepal. Retired Gurkha officers man the two recruiting camps — Dharan in eastern Nepal and Pokhara in the west. Special roaming scouts known as Galla Wallas, also Gurkha pensioners, comb far-off hillside villages, selecting promising youths for the recruiting sessions, much like football scouts searching for talent. When the time comes, thousands of young hopefuls begin a nationwide pilgrimage to become a

Lahure, or "go for a soldier." Up and down mountains, through freezing whitewater rivers, over fields and dusty trails, they journey on foot sometimes for as long as twenty days.

After a gruelling series of physical tests and interviews, the officers decide if a young hopeful is *nuckali suckali*, or "the right stuff" for the Gurkhas. The few chosen will be sent to Hong Kong for basic training and can barely contain their joy. Those rejected will try again next time, or will resume walking to join one of the Gurkha regiments that went to the Indian army after that country's independence.

Celebrating war's end, South Atlantic, 1982.

Joining the British army is for most Nepalese the chance of a lifetime. After fifteen or so years of service, the Gurkha soldier is eligible for a pension program that is administered with quasi-religious efficiency by the British army. Some Gurkha officers serve for nearly a lifetime, while their families become deeply connected to the British culture. Such was the case of Officer Cadet Bijay Kumar Rawat who in 1981 was presented the Sword of Honor at Sandhurst, given to the best overall officer cadet.

Officers in charge of Gurkha regiments are British, and aside from having to speak Gurkhali, as Nepalese is called in the army, they need to understand the subtle characteristics of the Gurkha mind. If successful, an officer will lead the best soldiers he could ever expect. A young New Zealander at Sandhurst once returned his posting request with the following choices; 1. A Gurkha regiment 2. A Gurkha regiment 3. A Gurkha regiment.

The Gurkha soldier expects his officer to measure up to his standards, and most generally do. When the Brunei emergency broke out in 1962, Major General Sir Walter Walker, the Gurkha general commanding officer, was off in the Himalayas visiting Gurkha pensioners, a five-day march from the nearest airfield. Once alerted to events, in true Gurkha style, he managed a forced, five-day-in-one march and was picked up by a Dakota twenty-four hours later.

Gurkhas are deeply religious. Some are Hindus, some are Buddhists, while others are animists. They all believe, however, there is no changing or escaping their destiny. This perhaps explains their unquestioning loyalty and resilience. Orders are almost sacred to Gurkhas. A young soldier posted on the Suez Canal during the First World War held a Royal Navy man-of-war at gunpoint until his officers arrived to countermand the order. In a river crossing in India during WWII, Brigadier Mark Tavershaw was forced to dive into the river to rescue a Gurkha Bren gunner who held tenaciously to his weapon as it sank to the bottom. He grasped the gun with such force that both men almost drowned before the Englishman was finally able to wrestle him to the surface. The Gurkha had been ordered never to abandon his weapon. In Burma, although ordered to destroy their heavy weapons, a Gurkha mortar squad refused and manhandled their mortar, all parts and ammunition throughout the 500-mile (800-kilometer) march.

The legendary zeal for one's weapons has raised several legends about the Gurkha kukri, the short, curved knife with the cutting edge on the inside and a notch above the hilt which allows the Gurkha to trap an enemy's blade and with a twist disarm him. Used as general purpose knives, the kukris are, however, fantastic close-combat weapons.

In the Arno Valley during the WWII Italian campaign, Lance Naik Jitbahadur Rai of the 1/7th Gurkhas, a small man even by Gurkha standards, led his men on a charge against German lines. With his kukri, he managed to kill two large Germans whose bodies fell over him, trapping him underneath. A third German charged into the melee, but Jitbahadur with great effort was able to free his right arm and slashed at the advancing enemy, almost chopping the German's arm off. Finally the small Gurkha NCO was freed by his men and the German taken prisoner. British officers on the scene were much amused as they saw the large German being brought into camp on a stretcher with the tiny Gurkha walking alongside him, bloody kukri in hand, patting the terrified German on the shoulder and telling him he was safe now . . . in Gurkhali.

Patrolling the British colony of Hong Kong, fighting in the South Atlantic, training in tough jungles of Belize and Brunei and performing their impeccable marching drill in all corners of the globe, the Gurkhas continue to honor their badge of the crossed kukris and their ancient saying, from the distant mountains of Nepal, *"Kaphar hunnu bhanda marnu ramro!"* "It is better to die than be a coward!"

(Previous Spread) The Grenadier Guards march past the queen upon receiving new colors. (This Page Top) Bearskins to the sky, the guards give three cheers to their sovereign. (Facing) The Irish Guards are the only regiment in the Household Division allowed to have a mascot. Connor MacNessa shown here is the ninth Irish wolfhound to serve the regiment.

The Scots Guards' corps of pipers maintains Scottish traditions such as use of the Tartan kilt and feather bonnet, along with the dirk, the Scottish knife, and the Piob Mhor or Great Highland bagpipe. Some accounts claim that when bonnie Prince Charles invaded England in the 1740s, he was mounted on a white stallion and preceded by more than seven hundred pipers. At the Jacobite defeat at Culloden several pipers were captured. One of them, James Reid, pleaded pardon saying he did not bear arms. The court ruled that since no Highland regiment ever went to battle without a piper, the bagpipe was in fact a weapon. Piper Reid was hanged.

Countless are the stories of pipers who led their men to battle risking enemy fire, and many were the besieged garrisons that heard the distant pipes of the relief forces giving them hope to resist their enemies. Pipers were present as recently as the Falklands/Malvinas War and at the war in the Persian Gulf.

The Lifeguards joined the Blues in 1939 to form the Household Cavalry. Thirty years later the First Royal Dragoons were incorporated into the Blues, forming the Blues and Royals. Mounting the guard at Whitehall Palace, they are the cavalry outfit of the Household Division.

LONDON CENTRAL
RM 194

(Previous Spread) The Tower of London is perhaps the greatest repository of British tradition. (This Page) The state dress is only used on special occasions. (Facing) Normally the blue undress uniform from Victorian times is worn. (Above) For more than seven hundred years without interruption, the Yeomen Warders have carried out the Ceremony of the Keys.

A charming story tells of the first time the Gurkhas saw Buckingham Palace. Detailed to participate in the 1953 coronation of Queen Elizabeth, the Gurkhas were ordered to form up for a practice run held at dawn which involved marching the route they would later cover. As they passed in front of the palace, the senior Gurkha officer ordered the men to march on tiptoe as not to awaken the young queen.

Coming from the hardships and poverty of the Himalayas, the Gurkhas possess a wonderful spirit and toughness. Trusting their beloved kukris (below), they are a perfect combination of old ways with modern adaptability. Well equipped with modern SA-80 rifles and machine guns, the Gurkhas are among the best fighting forces in history.

Music is a part of Gurkha tradition. Hillside shepherds fashion wooden flutes to idle away the time spent looking over their herds. The Scots, who are Britain's mountain men, have created an unbreakable bond with the nimble Nepalese after several joint actions, such as at the Battle of Dargai in India when they volunteered to carry Gurkha wounded. In the process they have taught the Gurkhas the drums and pipes. On regiment guest night, in true Highland tradition, Gurkha pipers march around the officer's table filling the decked-up mess with the shrill of the pipes. In war, the pipers and drummers serve as first-aid men and stretcher bearers to the regiment.

EIIR
7TH
DUKE OF EDINBURGH'S
OWN GURKHA RIFLES
2ND BATTALION
EGYPT 1915
SHARON
MEGIDDO
PALESTINE 1918
CTESIPHON
BAGHDAD
AFGHANISTAN 1919
7TH GURKHA

INDIA
Defenders of the Subcontinent
The President's Bodyguard
61st Cavalry

India has always been a land of lore and legend, a country-continent populated by masses of people of extraordinarily varied ethnic origins. Before the arrival of the European trading powers in the sixteenth century, India already had regular armies. The first recorded data of military significance comes from approximately 1500 BC when migrating white-skinned Aryans invaded the Indus Valley over the Hindu Kush. Driving the Dravidians, who inhabited northern India, to the south, the Aryans established the base of much of India's subsequent civilization.

Classical Indian armies were well organized and included four basic elements: the infantry, cavalry, a corps of chariots, and war elephants. The war elephants were extremely important in siege warfare and in attaining breakthrough during pitched confrontations. Led by the *mahut* (driver), the elephants each carried two or three men — armed with darts, bows and arrows, and the infamous *tomara* lance — in a wicker basket. Sometimes the elephants' tusks were sharpened for use as weapons or were lengthened with swords. They were used to produce shock, to ford streams and rivers, as moveable bridges, and in storming heavily defended positions where they could remove palisades with their strong trunks or ram gates, opening the way for infantry. Enemy cavalry was also affected by the elephants; both horses and men were terrified of the huge animals. While the large bulls were used in actual combat, cows and smaller bulls were employed in logistics, often in large trains to support advancing armies.

Even though only those from the warrior castes, known as the *ksatryia* class, could carry weapons according to the intricate caste system, armies of early India often numbered more than one million men. Most served as porters, grooms, armorers, and water bearers.

Parts of northern India were conquered by the Persians under Darius I toward the end of the sixth century BC. In 327-325 BC Alexander the Great entered northern India. He had met Darius

The Viceroy's Body Guard circa 1890.

at Gaugamela in Mesopotamia and, through small raids on the enemy camp, kept the Persians awake all night while his own troops slept. Victory was swift the following morning.

The Macedonians also met the large army of King Porus of the Paurava Dynasty of Punjab at the banks of the Hydaspes (now Jhelum) in July 326 BC. After tricking the Indians into deploying several times in many different directions, Alexander crossed the bulk of his troops away from his main camp under cover of a fierce thunderstorm. A first move by Porus to attack the bridgehead was checked by Alexander's central Asian horse-mounted archers, who forced the Indians back after their war chariots became caught in the mud. Porus advanced on the Macedonians without losing time, deploying his troops in classical Indian fashion with cavalry and chariots on the flanks and the shock of more than two hundred elephants and his massed infantry in the center. The Indian archers, however, were unable to find a stable footing for their longbows on the muddied ground. Again Alexander's horse archers proved decisive. A cavalry confrontation went to the Macedonians.

Sensing that his troops were in trouble, Porus dispatched his war elephants with mighty trumpets blaring and war drums rumbling across the battlefield. To the Macedonians they seemed like "a city on the move," but Alexander's phalanx stood firm with their long-shafted pikes and held back the elephants, slowly pushing them back with battle axes, although with tremendous casualties. Finally defeating the great beasts, the Macedonians set upon the Indian infantry, while the now free cavalry closed in from both flanks. Victory was complete. But reports of further Indian troops supported by thousands rather than hundreds of elephants made Alexander decide to return home.

The Mauryan and Gupta empires flourished from 320 BC until about AD 500, when an era of invasions by Huns, Muslims from Arabia, Persia, and Afghanistan and the Mongols ensued. The Mongols were led by Tamerlane who burned Delhi. Zahir-ud-din Muhammad or Babur (the Tiger), a Muslim ruler who was Tamerlane's great-grandson on his mother's side and Genghis Khan's relative on his father's, began the great Mogul Empire, conquering most of northern India. When he encountered the Rajput sultan of Delhi, Ibrahim Lodi, with 40,000 troops against his 25,000, Babur prepared a defensive wall formed by more than 700 wooden carts tied together. The two forces stood poised for eight days, taunting each other and daring one another to attack. Finally the sultan's troops charged, only to be stopped at the carts by a fierce defensive action which eventually pushed the attackers back and won the day.

The road to Delhi was open to Babur, whose family continued his conquests well after his death in 1530. The sixteenth century saw the arrival of Portuguese explorers followed by Dutch, English, and French traders. While the Europeans fought each other for control of trade with the subcontinent, the Mogul Empire finally came to an end, leaving India devoid of a strong centralized government.

In the mid 1700s, the British forced the French out of the race. In 1757 a handful of British soldiers and British-trained Indian troops, led by Robert Clive, defeated a 50,000-strong Maratha army at the Battle of Plassey (Palasi) through modern battle tactics and trickery (the British had bought off many of the Maratha generals). The East India Company soon became the leading power in virtually all of India. However, not all of the subcontinent gave in to the British, who had to fight several bloody wars against the Sikhs in the Pun-

Two Indian sowars, late nineteenth century.

jab and particularly on the savage northwest frontier. At the Battle of Aliwal, in which the Sikhs were decisively defeated, British veterans of Waterloo commented on the bravery of their Sikh adversaries.

The Mahrattas also resisted the British, who had to fight three bloody wars to subdue them. Although tough and bloody, British control over India had slowly produced loyal local troops recruited among the so-called martial classes. They were trained and led in the British manner, soaking up the traditions still seen today in India's military ceremonial. Indian troops saw action worldwide on behalf of the British. In China the first troops arriving to relieve the fifty-five-day siege of Peking by the Boxer hordes were Indian colonials.

The Sepoy Rebellion of 1857-1858 was the beginning of the Indian independence process, which saw a pause only during the two world wars, in which Indian soldiers wrote numerous pages of bravery.

At the outset of World War I, the Indian army counted 155,423 men. It would finish the Great War with 573,484 men in its ranks. Poorly equipped, carrying rifles the British had long since discarded, and trained only as auxiliaries to the British regiments, two Indian corps were thrown into the slaughter of France and Belgium at the end of 1914. Along with a motley group of British regulars and part-time territorials, these soldiers, albeit with tremendous casualties, held back the enemy onslaught until Lord Kitchener could train and equip his new British army.

In Palestine, Indian troops helped the British under Allenby push the Turks from the Sinai, through Lebanon, to Mesopotamia. Indian troops also fought in East Africa, in Salonika, and in the Dardanelles where along with other British and commonwealth troops they suffered tremendous casualties in the hell of Gallipoli.

In World War II Indian troops initially were sent to the Western Desert and Eritrea, where they rapidly gained the respect of their German and Italian foes. But the Indians eventually found themselves fighting closer to home. Again, India entered the war with outdated equipment, but as the conflict wore on, Indian soldiers proved their worth in all aspects of war. In Europe, Indian soldiers fought consistently well, particularly in Italy where the Indian assault on Cassino is much remembered. In Burma, Malaya, and Singapore, the Indian sepoy fought the highly skilled Japanese army and, even though they suffered initial setbacks, they bounced back to push the Imperial army away from their frontiers toward the sea to the south. Although much is said about crack American or British troops, such as Merrill's Marauders and the Chindits, out of one million Allied fighting men holding back the Japanese in Southeast Asia, more than 700,000 were Indian sepoys. The Indian fighting man emerged from WWII as a much respected warrior.

Indian independence in 1947-48 brought a new geopolitical buildup in the subcontinent. Immediately upon birth and partition, Hindu India faced war with the Muslim state of Pakistan, its newly formed neighbor, whose two portions flanked her. In 1948, the Indian army fought off a Pakistani-led insurgency of Pathan rebels in Kashmir, beginning a full-scale war between the two infant nations. The result was inconclusive and the area was turned into a "hot" border which remains volatile to this day.

The Indian army retained British-Indian traditions, and victories gained under British rule against Indians as well as foreign enemies continued to be commemorated by surviving regiments. In the 1960s, the Indian army mounted a successful offensive against the Portuguese enclave of Goa but suffered a serious setback against the Chinese on the northern Himalayan border.

In September 1965, border friction over Kashmir once again erupted between India and Pakistan. Lasting for about twenty-one days, the war was again fought to a stand off, although both sides showed improved professionalism in many fields. In the 1965 Indo-Pak War, Indian tanks sprang a cunning trap for a large force of Pakistani tanks at the village of Assal Uttar, on the northwest plains near the market town of Khem Karan.

Rapidly falling back, the Indian Centurion tanks slowly lured the superior Pakistani M47 and M48 Pattons toward a large horseshoe-shaped depression just outside the village which they had inundated by breaching irrigation ditches and dikes. Forcing the Pakistanis to maneuver through tall fields of sugar cane, the Indians placed themselves in hull-down position and fired at the waving sugar cane, just a few feet below the machine guns and radio aerials barely visible above the foliage. The attackers never knew what hit them as their vision was completely blocked. A total of ninety-seven first-line tanks were destroyed or captured at the Battle of Assal Uttar, which became known as the "*Patton-nagar*" or "Patton graveyard."

In 1971, India's army was much better trained and equipped. In a lightning strike that included joint operations and special forces strikes, the Indians supported a rebellion in eastern Pakistan that eventually created the sovereign nation of Bangladesh. Within twelve days, the Indian army had clinched the campaign in the east and held back a desperate Pakistani attack in the west, planned to disrupt Indian advances toward Dacca. With the fall of the city, the war rapidly came to an end as an undisputed Indian victory.

Today, the Indian army is rapidly growing to become a significant military power in the region. Almost one million strong, it faces a number of internal and external threats. The border disputes with Pakistan and China remain open, while internally terrorist emergencies in Kashmir, the Punjab, the Burmese frontier, and occasional serious bouts of Hindu-Muslim strife erupt. Recently, Indian troops have projected force in highly professional actions in

Indian cavalry on the western front. WWI.

the Maldive Islands and against brutal Tamil (Tiger) terrorists in Sri Lanka. Rarely does a day go by in which Indian troops are not engaged in combat in some corner of the vast subcontinent. Aside from adding numerous battle honors to the various Indian regiments, the military engagements have been turning the Indian army into one of the most experienced and battle-hardened forces in the world.

The President's Body Guard

British military tradition blends beautifully with proud Indian style in the modern-day ceremonial units such as the President's Bodyguard and the 61st Cavalry Regiment. Handpicked from the whole of India's army, the President's Bodyguard, stationed just outside the majestic Presidential Palace in New Delhi, is responsible for the security, escort, and ceremonial duties of the Indian president, and foreign dignitaries.

Raised in September 1773 by Warren Hastings,the then Governor of Bengal,the Governor General's Bodyguard,as it was called in British colonial times,is the senior-most regiment and corps of the Indian Army . They were first known as the Governor's Troop of Moguls. Composed of local *sowars* or cavalrymen, the GGBG served with distinction during the 1845-46 Sikh Wars and remained loyal throughout the Indian mutiny. Battle honors were various including Java, Ava, Maharajapore, Moodkee, Ferozeshah, Aliwal, and Sobraon, among others. PBG troops are the modern-day descendants of famous Indian cavalry units such as Skinner's Horse, Hodson's Horse, Gardner's Horse, and several other heavy and light cavalry and lancer units.

Serving the British governor general, these Indian troops wore wonderful scarlet tunics and measured at least six feet (1.83 meters) in height, forming a handsome troop indeed. In fact, an unofficial translation of the GGBG acronym was "God's Gift to Beautiful Girls." Today, the Indian army's PBG is formed by representatives of several of India's social castes who have done exceedingly well in service. The delicate nature of Indian politics and the proximity of the guards to the heads of state demands tough screening and complete confidence in a PBG member. The number of campaign and bravery medals pinned to the scarlet tunics of these tough-looking men attests to their merit. Aside from possessing a special demeanor and typical Indian aloofness, the members of the President's Bodyguard must be expert horsemen and have advanced parachute and tank training.

Clad in bright red *kurtalis* or tunics, with two rows of gold buttons down the front, and their distinctive turbans, known in Urdu as *lungis*, in winter or in their white full dress uniform in summer, the PBG troopers are among the most elegantly dressed in the world. Few are the officers and NCOs assigned to the PBG who do not sport several campaign medals, aside from the parachute wings which they wear on the right breast.

Many sport the winged dagger of special operations units, very similar to that worn by the British SAS but with markings in Urdu rather than English. Weapons consist of bamboo lances, tipped with the cavalry red and white banners, and sabers, both used in the fantastic cavalry drills in which the troopers demonstrate their incredible prowess on horseback. The uniform is completed with white gloves and breeches and long shiny black polished jackboots. Officers wear golden aiguillettes. The commandant of the regiment wears a beautiful uniform with a single central row of buttons and expertly embroidered facings on his tunic. An embroidered red and gold sabretache which was used in the eighteenth century to keep indispensable equipment (the uniform had no pockets) hangs by the sword. The commandant's horse sports a magnificent Indian saddle adorned with embroidered regimental badge and draped with a leopard's skin. Mounted on well-bred bays (with the exception of the trumpeters, who mount white horses in order to be seen by all in battle) and escorting one of several stately coaches used on official occasions, the President's Bodyguard embodies the military elegance of India's army.

61st Cavalry

Another of India's elite cavalry units is the 61st Cavalry. Based in the pink city of Jaipur on the fringes of the great western deserts south of Delhi, they claim their ancestry from the old Katchwaha Horse of the twelfth century. In fact, the modern unit was formed after independence in 1947 as an amalgamation of all the traditional Indian cavalry regiments and state forces, such as the Jodhpur Lancers, Mysore Lancers, Jenk Jamun & Kashmir Lancers, Soharaste Lancers, and the Gawlior Lancers. Thus, as is the PBG, they are composed of representatives of practically all of India's social strata, easily noticed by the format of the individual lungis denoting their respective castes.

Dressed in dark blue tunics with red facings and white crossbelt, the uniform of the 61st Cavalry also includes the exquisite gold, blue, and red lungi and gold cummerbunds worn underneath the white belts. A badge of the two-headed mythical Indian bird, the *garuda*, worn on the collar completes this striking uniform. The 61st also wears an olive green field uniform with turban and puttees similar to that worn by Indian troops in the First World War. An Enfield rifle is carried in a specially designed casing on the horse's side.

In khaki version of that uniform, elements of the 61st performed one of the last cavalry charges against a heavily fortified Turkish position on the Heights of Haifa in Palestine during WWI. Led by Major Dabat Singh, the Indian sowars swam their horses across the river at the base of a bluff while Turkish machine gunners rained fire on them from above. Charging repeatedly despite unbelievable casualties, the Indian cavalry finally reached the top of the bluff, successfully dislodging the Turks and gaining a glorious if bloody victory. The daring major, one of the numerous dead, won a posthumous Victoria Cross for his bravery in battle.

Elegant, proud, and professional, the Indian army through the surefooted steps of its dazzling cavalry shows that it has matured into one of the most well prepared forces in all of Asia.

-(Spread) The President's Bodyguard is formed from handpicked members of India's army — most are highly decorated combat veterans. (Above) Detail of the *lungi*, which is worn in a different manner by each of India's ethnic groups. The PBG includes Sikhs, Jats and Rajputs in its ranks. The uniform and accoutrements of India's senior-most regiment and corps are unchanged for over 120 years. Officers use shorter coats than their Junior Commissioned counterparts as well as the Sabretache. Horses must be a minimum 15 hands high and are the only ones in the Indian army with the right to wear manes. Elaborate Shabraques, sheep or panther skin covers, chain reins, white cords, throat ornaments and white brow bands comprise their ceremonial equipage.

"BHARAT MATA KI JAT" — Glory to Mother India is the unit's proud credo. (Top) The commandant of the President's Bodyguard flanked by standard bearer, trumpeters, and officers of his troop. The elephant, besides being the image of India's strength and resilience, was the mighty backbone of India's ancient armies. (Right) Members of the PBG often display their expert horsemanship. (Above) Staff car.

-(Left) Detail of the commandant's richly decorated saddle and sabretache, a piece of military equipment used by the Hussars in the eighteenth century and rarely seen today. (Bottom) The President's Bodyguard parades into the Presidential Palace in Delhi. Riding from the India Arch in the background to the Presidential Palace, the PBG is one of Delhi's most fantastic sights.
- The summer uniform of the President's Bodyguard is entirely white and buttoned single brested in contrast with the two rows of golden buttons in the red coat.

The 61st Cavalry was formed to represent all the traditional Indian cavalry corps of the past. (Facing Spread) Hailing from Jaipur, India's pink city on the fringe of the desert, the 61st Cavalry is formed by expert horsemen. (Above) Trumpeters ride white horses to be readily seen in battle. Note the two-headed *garuda* badge on the trumpet banner.

DENMARK
The Guards
The Royal Life Guards

Copenhagen is Denmark's heart and soul. A modern center of commerce and industry, it attracts visitors from all over the world with its lively street life, charming architecture, and the world-famous Tivoli Gardens. Yet if one image truly defines the spirit of Denmark, it would be the Royal Livgarde, Denmark's Royal Life Guards.

Every day at noon, a detachment leaves the gates of the guards' barracks next to Rosenborg Palace and marches down the city center to relieve the guardsmen at Amalienborg, the royal residence. Traffic cautiously finds its way around them, children follow excitedly, shopkeepers greet them with proud smiles, and tourists stop in their tracks at the uncommon sight of elegantly clad guardsmen trudging down the city's thoroughfares. The guards stop at attention at red traffic lights. When the light turns green, they resume marching in a wonderfully unassuming way. At no point along their march do they disturb the daily routine of their capital, into which they fit perfectly. A crowd is waiting as they enter the palace courtyard. The guards proceed with the intricate ceremony of replacing the old guard, who, after twenty-four hours on duty, marches off to the barracks by the same route.

The Royal Livgarde was formed by King Frederick III in June 1658. Denmark was still nursing the wounds of the 1657 Swedish invasion when word came of a new landing at Korsør, Zealand, in early August, only a month after the guard was formed. The invading army of Charles X sped toward Copenhagen, hoping to topple the Danish government and strengthen Sweden's grasp on the strategic Baltic waters. The 550 guardsmen, forming about one-fifth of all available Danish troops, hastily prepared to defend the city. The Swedes set up camp just outside the besieged walls while their fleet blockaded the Oresund. In February 1659 the Swedes finally attacked. After listening to reports on the brutality of the Swedish advance, King Frederick decided the situation had gone too far and said, "I will die in my nest." Rallied by the guards, the entire population fought back. While able-bodied men held the forward positions, older men, women, and children poured water down the frosty stones of the city ramparts, making it impossible for the Swedes to scale the walls. The Livgarde conducted counterattacks, demolished approach trenches, and raided the enemy's forward positions. The Swedes never entered Copenhagen. With the arrival of an allied Dutch fleet and reinforcements from Holland, the Danes slowly pushed the invaders back. The Livgarde had truly been born in battle. A thankful King Frederick decided that from that moment forward the guard would also provide direct security for the royal family.

The Danish Army defeats the Prussians at Isted.

In 1675 the Danes attempted an invasion of Skane, landing at several beachheads in southern Sweden. Although Adm. Niels Juel's fleet decisively defeated the Swedish navy at sea, the Danes were unable to match those successes on land. In 1676 the Swedes

The Guards march past. Late 19th century.

defeated the Danish troops at the Battle of Lund. Under terrible cannon fire and freezing cold, the Livgarde covered the retreat of the Danish army. Meanwhile Danish guards were also fighting in Germany alongside King William III of Orange in the Third Dutch War. They saw action against King Louis XIV's French guards in Flanders and participated in several battles in Ireland, including Boyne, Limerick, and Athlone. The Livgarde also fought beside the Duke of Marlborough at Blenheim, Oudenarde, and Malplaquet in the War of the Spanish Succession. In the Great Northern War of 1709-20, a combined Russo-Danish and Polish army defeated Sweden's troops under Charles XII. The Livgarde assisted in the battles in Skane and in northern Germany. Sweden's supremacy of the Baltic was finally toppled, and Copenhagen was no longer lying exposed on the enemy border.

During the Napoleonic Wars, Denmark was coerced by the French to join in an alliance against Sweden and Great Britain. The Danish fleet was the third most powerful in Europe, and the Royal Navy immediately blockaded Copenhagen and bombarded the city. Knowing that the bulk of the Danish army was stationed in Holstein to protect their southern flank from a French "change in spirits," British forces landed in northern Zealand just fifteen miles (twenty-five kilometers) from Copenhagen. The Danes put up a stiff defense but the rising number of civilian casualties forced them to surrender. The British made away with the Danish fleet as they had with the

The Guards served in battledress during World War Two.

Spanish ships at Cadiz. A cannon ball embedded in the outer wall of the guards' barracks at Rosenborg remains a vivid reminder of the siege.

In 1848 the mostly German populations of the Duchies of Schleswig and Holstein revolted against Danish rule. The revolt escalated into full-scale war. Soon Danish troops were battling the German army on the European mainland. The two-year war culminated with the great Danish victory at the Battle of Isted on 25 July 1850. The battle was the largest in Scandinavia, with nearly 60,000 troops involved. After a confused and bloody morning, the Livgarde tried a frontal attack against a three-cannon battery which was firing shrapnel to hold back the Danish advance. Finally overwhelming the German defenders, the guards took the six-pounders and turned them against the enemy almost immediately. Despite a fierce German counterattack, the guards held their position and instigated a sudden offensive, breaking the enemy's determination. The guards pursued the enemy through the mists of Isted Forest until the battlegrounds were once again silent.

It was at Isted that the Danish army captured a large number of first-class infantry sabers that are used by the Livgarde to this day. Made in Versailles, France, they were originally the standard infantry sidearm of Napoleon's army, Sabre Briquet model IX or XV in reference to the French Revolutionary calendar. In 1815 they were captured by the Prussians at Waterloo and became the German army's standard infantry weapon, the Infanterie Seite Gewehr 1818 (Infantry Sidearm 1818). At Isted the Danes captured 2,340 sabers and 544 went to the Livgarde, who shrewdly hid them from the Nazi Germans in 1943 and still wear them proudly today. The blue dress uniform with bearskin hat is also reminiscent of the Danish-German wars.

A second Schleswig-Holstein war followed in 1864, resulting in the Danish cession of the two territories to a much reinforced Prussian-Austrian force. At Dybøl, the Livgarde put up a stubborn two-month defense but was eventually overcome after sustaining 3,000 casualties.

During World War I, Denmark remained in a state of armed neutrality, having mined the Baltic straits and placed heavy naval batteries throughout the strategic seashore. Too many years of peace, however, gave the Danes a false feeling of security which would prove deadly on 9 April 1940. Operation Weseruebung, the combined taking of Denmark and Norway by Nazi Germany, began with an airborne assault on the Stoerstrom bridge which linked the island of Falster to Zealand and Copenhagen. Another successful drop assured Nazi control of Denmark's major airfield at Aalborg. Two hours later, Luftwaffe fighters were operating from the airfield while German Panzers rapidly closed in on the capital. The first airborne operation in history took the Danish forces completely by surprise. Although sporadic resistance was put up in Jutland, the Livgarde detachment at the royal palace in Copenhagen was soon battling in the streets against advanced patrols of the Wehrmacht. As gunfire echoed outside, King Christian X continued addressing his War Council inside the building.

Due to the complete surprise, a cease-fire was arranged, stopping the German advance mere blocks from Amalienborg Palace. For a few years, German occupation allowed the regiment to maintain guard duty at Amalienborg, but gradually pressure increased as resistance movements became better organized. Many guardsmen had fled to resume fighting with other free nations, and a full Livgarde brigade was formed in Sweden to fight back at the first opportunity. When notified that the use of a yellow star over the left breast had been mandatory for all Danish Jews, King Christian said, "If they have to wear it, then I'll wear it, too." Immediately the Danish population joined together in finding ways to help Danish Jews out of the country. Through a network of fishermen, truck drivers, bureaucrats, and a myriad of others, most were removed to England or Sweden and successfully avoided the danger faced by Jews in other occupied countries.

Danish resistance waged a furious undercover war against their Nazi oppressors, attacking strategic targets, destroying railroads, factories, shipping, ammunition and petrol stockpiles, and targeting traitors and high-ranking enemy officers. Guardsmen manned the top posts in the undercover intelligence network, many using the cover of their daily duties guarding the king.

On 29 August 1943, the Nazis unleashed a brutal assault against what remained of the Danish identity. The Livgarde barracks were surrounded and taken after fierce resistance by the guards on duty. Amalienborg was also taken, as was the summer palace of Sorgen Frai, where a dozen guardsmen held back hundreds of attackers, until they were overwhelmed. As the German general commanding the operation approached the king with an ultimatum, he was greeted with a sarcastic *"Guten tag, Mein Tapfrer General"* (Good morning, my brave general), which certainly must have deflated the commander's bravado.

Guardsmen were at the forefront of resistance fighters who cleaned the streets of Copenhagen upon liberation in May 1945. Since World War II, Danes have vowed "never to see a ninth of April again." Young guardsmen on combat training are taught guerrilla tactics and urban fighting techniques. They are as comfortable with wire-guided, portable anti-tank missiles as they are with Molotov cocktails. Denmark has also joined NATO and consistently keeps her troops battle-ready by sending contingents to several peace-keeping missions. More than 35,000 Danish troops have worn the blue beret of the United Nations in conflicts around the globe.

Today, the Royal Danish Life Guard remains a central part of Denmark's active army, aside from providing the sovereign's guard. Young conscripts come from all parts of Denmark hoping to be chosen for the 1,200-strong regiment. Serving in the Livgarde is a national honor, a legacy for life which can enhance a young man's social and professional acceptance. Many families have several generations of guardsmen, six being the record to date. Currently six brothers of one family are in the regiment, another certain record. Before donning the Blues and Bearskins, a young conscript must spend eight months in the field, where he endures a tough basic combat course, learning everything from infantry tactics and guerrilla warfare to survival tactics on the battlefield. Finally, when he is qualified as an efficient infantryman, he sheds his camouflaged fatigues and German Heckler & Koch G-3 rifle and receives his blue guardsman uniform and his M-1 Garand. This graduation takes place during a moving ceremony known as "The Blue Dinner," when new guardsmen and their families celebrate their right to defend the queen.

For the remaining four months of their national service, they will take to the streets of Copenhagen in Blues and Bearskins as did their forebears in the icy mists of Isted Forest.

"The youngest drummer boy reports to the drum major that the drum is broken" by Wilhelm Rosenstand. When this painting appeared at a Copenhagen auction, the Livgarde commander dispatched the regiment adjutant with the officers' funds to purchase it at any cost. At the auction, the adjutant was unable to outbid an elegant gentleman who took the painting home. The following day a much distressed adjutant had to explain to a raging commanding officer that the funds were insufficient. At that moment, however, a messenger arrived from the royal palace with a parcel containing the much valued painting and a card: "To the guards from King Friedrich X."

The Royal Danish Life Guard embodies the fighting spirit of a small but proud country. After tough basic training, the young conscripts spend countless days polishing boots and cartridge pouches with wax, water, cotton, and "elbow grease" until their image reflects in the leather. They drill endlessly with bearskin hats at the Livgarde barracks in Rosenborg. (Facing) Grizzly bearskins come from Canada and are strictly within conservation standards.

telefon
telefon
1658-1958

Since their Viking ancestors landed on British soil, the Danes have held the crown of England several times. They have headed a union of all the Scandinavian countries and once governed all the islands in the North Atlantic. Their power extended throughout the southern Baltic eastward to Estonia. They retained Norway until 1814 and rule over Greenland and the Faroes to this day. The Danes also founded trading stations in western Africa and in the East and West Indies. For more than four hundred years, they exacted dues from every ship entering or leaving the Baltic.

Guard duty is usually carried by thirty-six guardsmen, the band, and a corps of drums. (Facing) The blue tunic, reminiscent of the Danish-German Wars of 1848-50 and 1864, is double-breasted and buttoned to the right one month and to the left the next to reduce wear and tear. On very rare state occasions, a single-breasted scarlet tunic is worn. (Below) Guards stop for red lights.

DEN KONGELIGE LIVGARDE
VAGTKOMPAGNIET

29. August 1943

NM 23 591

GREECE
Of Thieves and Mountain Men
The Evzones

Classical Greece gave the western world a wide array of riches in knowledge, philosophy, architecture, science, and literature. In the military field it produced great genius among its organized and versatile warriors. Many of the tactics and strategies employed to this day have their origins in the Greek struggles for the bridge between East and West that they held onto tenaciously for so many centuries.

Greek military prowess fills volumes of lore and legend, from circa 1200 BC when Agamemnon of Mycenae commanded an army across the Aegean to rescue Helen, his brother's wife, from the hands of Paris, the son of King Priam of Troy. For nine years, the Greek army ravaged the northwestern Asia Minor land of Troy, unable to decisively breach the walls of the great city. In the tenth year, the Greeks tried a daring feint that would become the precursor of military diversion and dissimulation. An enormous hollow wooden horse, secretly filled with Greek soldiers, was offered to the Trojans as a divine gift. The Greek fleet then made sure it was seen setting sail for home. When the horse was pulled into the city walls, the fleet returned and, aided by the soldiers concealed inside the horse who opened the gates, the Greek army swiftly conquered the city.

The great city-states of Greece introduced several of the military techniques that have molded the way men fight wars. Their great reliance on naval forces and their use of embarked (marine) troops were described by Themistocles in the fifth century BC when he wrote that the Greek navy was "the wooden walls of Athens." Strict military training and discipline, reverence for their weapons and a moral code of valor were the trademarks of Spartan warriors. Young Spartans were engaged at age seven and learned to keep and maintain their weapons. When handed their shields they were reminded to "come back with it or come back lying on it." At the Battle of Thermopylae (480 BC) an elite force of three hundred Spartans led by Leonidas held back the Persians in a heroic stand on

Evzones fight the Turks in the trenches.

a mountain pass, allowing most of the Greek army to escape. On the monument built after the struggle a simple phrase marked for generations the valorous spirit of these troops: "Go tell Sparta that we fell according to its laws."

Special Forces and covert operations also owe their beginnings to the ancient Greeks. In the Peloponnesian Wars special troops known as the *yinnites* (the nude ones) and the *psiloi* (the thin ones), clad only in loin cloths and carrying light swords and slings,

Greek troops dance the Chamikos in the First Balkan War.

were sent on covert missions behind enemy lines, disrupting water supplies with conium and arsenic and burning stores of cereals. These troops usually linked up with spies who operated extensively inside enemy territory.

Another Greek innovation was the use of codes and signals. The town of Michennes just west of Athens was informed in just under one and a half days of the fall of Troy, more than 350 miles (600 kilometers) away, through the use of fractories, signal fires lit on islands and high vantage points in an intricate communication network.

The most celebrated battle of classical Greece occurred on the plain of Marathon in the year 490 BC. A large Persian force was met by the Greek troops led by Miltiades who shrewdly avoided contact, slowly drawing the Persians toward a reconnoitered area of swamps. Once the enemy was trapped in the best tactical location, the *hoplites* (citizen soldiers) of Athens pounced, destroying them. After the swift victory, the Greeks detached the runner Pheidippides to inform Athens of the victory. Laden with shield, sword, helmet, and shin armor, he ran the twenty-seven miles (forty-four kilometers) to Athens where he was only able to whisper, "*Nenikikamen*," "We have won!" before perishing of exhaustion. From that brave feat the Marathon race is still run to this day.

In 334 BC on the small, poor, semi-civilized mountain kingdom of Macedon, on Greece's northern border a great warrior began the creation of a fantastic empire and traced a new direction in the ways of waging war. Alexander the Great organized his army through leadership by example, trust, loyalty, and honor. He introduced decent pay, ensured care, responsibility for the wounded, and honor for the dead. He made sure the widows and orphaned children of his soldiers were taken care of, and that his troops were well tended through every hardship.

In the field he pioneered great innovations, such as siege machines, like the capricorn, a heavy ramming device to bring down fortified gates; and siege towers, which placed his archers on an equal footing with city ramparts. These were generally covered with wet cowskins, which ensured protection against burning arrows. Primitive catapults date from this period as does the phalanx, a solid and concentrated mass of infantry whose tactical mission was to push the enemy's central line of battle not unlike the tank of today. Using eighteen-foot spears, the front lines advanced while every other man pushed and supported them. The phalanx moved only forward and obeyed a single order at a time. It was, however, flexible, being able to change from tetragon to rectangle at a given order or even split in half for two-pronged attacks. Alexander's phalanxes carved a vast empire that spread from Greece and the Middle East to northern India.

In 146 BC, Momius Pilatus captured all of Greece in the name of the mighty Roman Empire, an era which continued until Byzantine times. Greece under Constantine the Great saw the arrival of light and heavy cavalry, mainly the *katafracti* or cataphract heavy cavalry, the predecessor of the armed knights of the Middle Ages. A special secret weapon, used primarily against the Turks and Bulgars, was *igron pir* (liquid fire), a mixture of sulphur, asphalt, and other chemicals burned in stoves and fired in jets through pipes by a vacuum system. This highly effective weapon was commonly used at the bows of the *dromon* warships of the Greeks, as well as in forward defenses on land.

Constantinople, the enlightened center of the Byzantine world, fell to the Turks in 1453, casting Greece under four hundred years of Turkish occupation.

Throughout the occupation, the Greek population was never complacent. Local revolts were frequent, as were hit-and-run attacks throughout the mainland and the islands. Finally in 1821 widespread insurrection broke out from the Peloponnesus through Macedonia. Greek mercenaries known as the *armatoli* (those allowed to carry weapons) had the task of guarding the sultan's properties, such as street squares and fountains. They in fact used their military training to begin the insurrection in the mountains. They were promptly joined by the Klepths (mountain thieves) and inspired the people as the *palikari* (the brave ones) who waged daring guerrilla attacks on Turkish targets.

Greek Artillery bombards Bulgarian lines in 1913.

Evzone troops march out to the front. December 1916.

Soon the Greek army was able to face the Turks in set-piece battles and momentum began to grow. At the battle of Devernakia, the Ottoman general Dramali Passar was decisively defeated by the Greek generals Kolokotronis and Nikitaras who took advantage of the rough mountain terrain. Besides losing practically all of his forces, his entire harem was also captured by the beaming Greeks. From this motley crew of irregulars clad in the traditional garb of mountainfolk and bandits, many times carrying captured Turkish weapons, developed the Evzones, the first organized corps of the modern Greek army.

The Evzones, or Tsoliades as described by Homer, got their name from the special units of classical Greece who carried the heavy swords, shields, spears, and helmets, the word literally meaning, "the ones who are very well structured." After Greece's independence in 1832, the Evzones already made up half of the entire Greek infantry. Peace did not last long, however, and from 1904-1908 the Evzones were heavily involved in the Macedonian struggles against armed bands of Bulgars known as *komitadjis* (committees) who raided Greek settlements, trying to suppress any sign of Greek cultural coherence, killing teachers and Greek Orthodox priests, and going as far as moving nameplates and destroying crosses in cemeteries. It was a long and bitter war fought mostly in the swamps, mountains, and snows of Macedonia. This struggle inevitably led to the First Balkan War.

The two Balkan Wars (1912-13) finally secured all of Salonika for Greece and brought great losses for the Ottoman Empire. In just two years the Turks lost almost 80 percent of all their territories in the Balkans and most of their European population. Six Evzone battalions saw most of the fighting on the Greek side, which prepared them for World War I, where they joined the Serbs and French in defeating the joint coalition of Germany, Turkey, and Bulgaria. After the armistice, an Evzone battalion caused quite a stir as it marched into the Champs Elysées in the Allied victory parade.

World War II again saw Greek Evzones wearing their traditional mountain uniforms, first giving Benito Mussolini's troops a hard time in Albania and later clashing against a joint German-Italian force in home territory. Unable to counter the German blitzkrieg, Greek and British troops employed a series of desperate delaying actions until the final invasion of crack German and Italian Condor, Edelweiss, Alpini, and Folgore airborne and

The Evzones parade down the Champs Elysées. 1918.

mountain troops on Crete. Undaunted, the Greeks fought on as resistance guerrillas and in exile with the British in North Africa and Europe.

After WWII, the Greek army fought a bloody civil war against communist insurgents in 1944-49 and then participated in the Korean War as part of the United Nations contingent. In all of these actions the Evzones fought as front-line troops.

Today the Evzones serve as Greece's most visible soldiers. Garrisoned at the George Tzavella barracks adjacent to the Presidential Building in Athens, the 180 Evzones and one company of Cretan guards are responsible for the honor guard to the tomb of Greece's unknown soldier bordering Athens central Syntagma Square. They also guard the Presidential Building, participate in national festivities alongside the Greek president, and form a guard of honor for foreign dignitaries. On Sundays and holidays the Evzones are granted the supreme honor of raising and lowering the flag at the Acropolis and appear in their white ceremonial dress at the tomb of the unknown soldier.

Not all Greek soldiers can join the Evzones and the posting is much coveted. A minimum height of 6 feet (1.85 meters) must be accompanied by perfect health, unblemished character, and a good moral standing. Before learning the intricate routine and the complicated steps of the honor guard, all Evzones must pass combat basic training. Only then can they wear the "Blue and White" which symbolize Greece's sky and clouds, as well as the sea and the foam of the Aegean.

A mixture of all periods of Greek history makes up the Evzone uniform. The tight belt of Homer's "well-belted" warriors and the classical *fustanella* tunic or "toga" remind one of the classical period, while the gold embroidered waistcoat, white stockings, and cleated mountain shoe called *tsarouhia* come from the *palikari* of the eighteenth century. The *fario* hat is a common tasseled fez, inherited from the Turks, as is the short *vraka* scimitar used by the officers and the Cretans.

The Evzone uniforms are handmade by skilled mountain craftsmen according to Greek tradition. Each uniform takes almost 80 days to complete and no two are alike in their intricately embroidered details.

Today the ceremonial uniform and the Cretan Guards can only be seen on Sundays and holidays when great crowds turn up in front of Syntagma Square. For daily guard duties the Evzones wear their khaki (summer) or blue (winter) undress tunics over their stockings and tsarouhias. Their close precision rounds with intricate arm, leg, and rifle movements still mesmerize the tourists and passersby who gather every half hour to admire the modern day Evzones under the scorching sun of Greece.

The Evzones are a living reminder to Greeks of their independence from four hundred bitter years of Ottoman rule. (Preceding spread) The intricate ceremony of the Mounting of the Guard takes place at the Tomb of the Unknown soldier honoring all Greek military dead since Hellenic times. Note the distinctive tsarouhia shoe, made of pig leather, decorated with red dye, and black woolen pom pom covering the final sewing. These rugged shoes were used extensively by Greek mountain men and today can only be made by one shoemaker in Greece. It has sixty cleats in the sole which create a distinctive sound and grip to steep mountain trails. The tsarouhia shoe became the symbol of Greece's struggle against the Germans and Italians and was used for climbing and kicking. In the Albanian campaign, several Evzones short of ammunition even bombarded advancing Italian troops with their tsarouhias. (Above) Evzones parade on a sunny Athens Sunday. Note the officers' stivalia boots of typically Turkish design.

Officers (Left facing) in the Evzones wear Red and Gold fermelis and carry the curved vraka scimitar which was often captured from dead Turks in battle during the 1821 War of Independence. The Evzones also include one company of Cretan Guards (Left) representing the Islands. The short fustanella kilt made of white cotton from a 35-yard (30-meter) long piece of cloth has four hundred pleats each symbolizing a bitter year of Turkish domination. Legend has it that Greek mountain men would add a pleat a year until 1821 when they finally gained independence.

All Evzones are above 6 feet (1.85 meters) in the tradition of the "well-belted" warriors of ancient Greece. Today swords and spears have been replaced by the ubiquitous U.S.-made Garand M-1 rifle. No two Evzone uniforms are identical. The flowing white ipoditis shirt and the lavishly embroidered fermeli waistcoat are of Turkish influence as is the red fario or fez symbolizing the blood in the struggle for liberation.

THE UNITED STATES OF AMERICA
The Brave

The United States Military Academy at West Point
The United States Third Infantry
The United States Marine Corps

From the beginning, American leaders have displayed an uncanny ability to rally their men through defeat and deprivation, instilling resilience which would ultimately bring victory. In the Revolution and throughout America's history, its fighting leaders have maintained the traditional standards of command, courage, and determination.

The colonists, formed into militias by the British government, saw extensive action in the French and Indian wars that ravaged North America for almost ten years. When the time came to take to arms against the British, the founding fathers formed the battle-hardened Continental army, an American institution that preceded the country itself. The army's "minutemen" were well-trained, "ready to fight at a minute's notice." With expertly aimed shots, they drove the British out of Lexington and Concord. The attempt to seize arms and munitions opened the eight-year revolutionary war. Of the eight hundred British Redcoats sent to disarm the patriot stocks in Concord, seventy-three were killed, 174 wounded, and twenty-six missing after the initial "shots heard around the world." Sharpshooting snipers, sworn to become independent, harassed them on their retreat to Boston.

Fighting was fierce and the hastily organized colonial army suffered immensely as it slowly built itself into a well-oiled fighting force. But the flame of independence shone through the bitter cold of Valley Forge and the resounding defeat at Monmouth, keeping the men fighting and the spirit alive. Foreign soldiers — such as the indomitable Prussian drillmaster Baron Friedrich Von Steuben, who pulled the motley troops together and wrote the first American military manual, and the young French Marquis de Lafayette — greatly enhanced the colonial army's fighting power.

Hit-and-run tactics and resolve provided a winning edge. The extraordinary Kentucky rifle enabled running militiamen to hit a six-inch (15.25-centimeter) target from more than two hundred yards (180 meters), a prowess unmatched by the British and their slow smoothbore muskets. With the decisive encounters at Saratoga in 1777 and Yorktown in the fall of 1781, America was finally able to stand on its own.

Throughout the long and tiring war, the colonists' bold tactics sapped the British resolve: Washington's Christmas crossing of the frozen Delaware River to surprise the greatly feared Hessian mercenaries at Trenton in 1776, and guerrilla strikes such as Ethan Allen and Benedict Arnold's Green Mountain Boys attack on Fort Ticonderoga and Francis "Swamp Fox" Marion's actions in the South. At 10 A.M. on 19 October 1781, British Redcoats, donning fresh tunics and marching to the tune of "The World Turned Upside Down," slowly laid their arms in a pile before the exultant colonists.

In the War of 1812, the British again attempted to subdue the colonies, initially gaining the upper hand against hastily assembled and untrained troops. Washington, D.C., was taken and the White House and Congress burned before Andrew Jackson's troops defeated the British in New Orleans. Never again would the American capital be taken by foreign troops. And never again would the United States forsake the need for a powerful, well-organized army.

Pushing west, the U.S. Army slowly gained territory from Indians and Mexicans. In 1836 at the Alamo in San Antonio, Texas, 188 Americans, including William Travis, Davy Crockett, and James Bowie, held back more than three thousand attacking Mexicans before being overwhelmed and slaughtered. Sixteen hundred enemy attackers were killed in the fray. The fighting spirit of the American frontiersman prevailed, however, and Texas rapidly wrested its independence from Mexico. With tremendous gains in western territories and growing industrial development, few Americans could foresee the approach of their greatest debacle, a conflict which would strike deep into the nation's soul: the Civil War of 1861-1865.

The first Confederate shells rained down on Charleston's Fort Sumpter in the spring of 1861. Brother against brother, the Blue and the Gray clashed in a five-year slaughter. The South's initial drive — with victories at Bull Run, Fredericksburg, and Chancellorsville — was finally halted by McClellan's Yankees at Antietam. A further rebel attempt in Pennsylvania through the Shenandoah Valley sparked the brutal three-day battle of Gettysburg, without a doubt the most important in the country's history, with more than 168,000 participants and 51,000 casualties.

Gettysburg marked the turning point of the Civil War. Southern casualties could not be replaced fast enough to resist Union generals Grant and Sherman on their drive south. Atlanta was burned and the South ravaged. The Union armies took Richmond and forced General Lee's surrender at Appomattox in April 1865.

The Civil War marked the impact of the industrial revolution on the realm of warfare. Railroads were used extensively to ferry troops to the front line. The Gatling, a primitive machine gun, made its debut on the Union side. Telegraph communications effectively enhanced command and control, and hot air balloons were used for aerial reconnaissance of enemy movements.

Irregular Southern troops initiated bold attacks on the unsuspecting Yankee rear with sudden fire and the terrifying rebel yell, only to disappear back into the brush before the confused enemy had time to react. Modern tactics were devised to decrease the incredible number of casualties. The bloody years of the secession split America in two.

Although surrounded by blood and the pressure of battle, many American soldiers and officers never lost their bravado. In October 1864, the rebel general J. B. Hood, surrounding a Union position at Ressaca, Georgia, demanded "the immediate and unconditional surrender of the post and garrison." He advised his Yankee counterpart that, "should this be acceded to, all white officers and soldiers will be paroled in a few days. If the place is carried by assault, no prisoners will be taken." Shortly thereafter, an aide arrived back with a small envelope containing the enemy's reply: "I am somewhat surprised at the concluding paragraph to the effect that if the place is carried by assault, no prisoners will be taken," stated the Union commander of the post, Clark R. Weaver. "In my opinion I can hold this post. If you want it, come and take it." More than 120 years later, another American, Brigadier General Anthony McAuliffe, encircled at the Belgian town of Bastogne by German Panzer divisions, would keep alight the flame of American defiance

Union troops of the 12th New York Infantry pose for the camera during the Civil War.

by replying to the enemy's surrender propositions in a similar mode. His short note simply read: "To the German Commander: NUTS! - the American Commander."

Time and again, America's "wild west" spirit won the day. The defeat of General George C. Custer's Seventh Cavalry by Cheyenne and Sioux Indians at Little Big Horn reminded settlers that the country's native people were still deeply imbued with the warrior spirit. Even so, the might of the country's army became more and more apparent. With Teddy Roosevelt's enthusiastic Roughriders leading the way up San Juan Hill, America became a worldwide power.

When the government decided to enter the fray of the First World War, more than two million young doughboys were drilled and equipped in a mere eighteen months to help push the Kaiser's armies back. With excited shouts of "Lafayette here we come!" fresh U.S. troops landed in France. Again, great leadership was available in the form of General John Joseph Pershing, who rapidly realized U.S. troops had to fight their own war rather than become replacements for depleted French and British forces. Fighting under their own command with fresh youthful spirit, America's victories mounted. Château-Thierry, Belleau Wood, the Marne, St. Mihiel, and Meuse-Argonne soon became streamers in regimental flags while the proud young soldiers marched toward Germany to the strains of "Over There."

Restrained from joining the second European conflict until 1941, U.S. troops found themselves incapable of holding back massive Japanese assaults throughout southern Asia. Yet, America's overwhelming industrial capacity and its spiritual resilience soon prevailed. A slow and bloody worldwide campaign alongside the Allies managed to push the Axis troops back throughout the globe. Operation Torch in North Africa secured the southern doorway into Europe, followed by landings in Sicily and a sweep up the Italian boot. The D-Day landings in Normandy opened a second front in the north, tracing the road to Belgium, Holland, and ultimately Germany. In the Far East, a brutal island-by-island struggle against the Japanese took the GIs across the Pacific to Iwo Jima and Okinawa, the doorsteps of Japan.

When the war ended, the United States emerged as a world superpower. Battle honors accumulated, and names such as Anzio, the Bulge, Corregidor, Normandy, Tarawa, Guadalcanal, Cassino, Iwo Jima, and Okinawa became deeply ingrained in American history.

The young GIs had barely returned stateside when a seemingly unimportant emergency in Korea escalated into a three-year quagmire. The spread of Communism started an undeclared "Cold War" where several isolated conflicts would be fought. In Vietnam, a Southeast Asian land of tropical highlands and rice paddies, the United States was forced to look deeply within. Fighting with politically restrained commitment, U.S. troops found it increasingly hard to defend the countryside from shrewd Viet Cong guerrilla veterans. Ever unpopular at home, the Vietnam War once again divided the country. Although small special forces units successfully defeated the Vietnamese in isolated areas of the country, the U.S. military was hit hard by the conflict.

America rapidly came to terms with defeat, albeit political, and worked fast and hard to regain its blemished respect. Out of the post-Vietnam catharsis that engulfed the military and the nation arose the mightiest fighting force the world has ever seen; wholly professional, superbly trained and equipped, versatile and specialized, and, as has generally been the case, extremely well led and motivated.

The United States Military Academy at West Point

Some fifty miles (eighty kilometers) north of New York City, the Hudson River suddenly snakes and narrows while bare granite bluffs drop from their heights and bite into the slow-moving waters. Today this tranquil river bend is but a vista for visitors at one of America's most revered institutions, but it was once one of the nation's most important defensive bastions. During the revolutionary war, General George Washington, recognizing the strategic significance of West Point, rapidly turned it into one of the Colonial army's first defensive positions. On 20 January 1778 a permanent garrison was stationed and armed to deter British shipping from gaining control of the river waters and physically splitting the colonies in two. An enormous iron chain was strung from West Point to Constitution Island to block the passage of any British vessel that succeeded in bypassing the position's guns. West Point's artillery commanded the exact spot where wind and current conditions forced enemy shipping to tack, causing the warships to be extremely slow and vulnerable to the cannonade. The British, not surprisingly, never came.

In July 1802, the United States Military Academy at West Point opened its gates to the first class of ten cadets, the first of thousands of America's military leaders. Slowly, the academy grew into a beautiful complex of buildings, parks, and monuments that embody countless feats of bravery by its sons. To visit West Point without feeling the heavy weight of history is impossible. At the stone gate marking the entrance to the academy grounds, a large engraved shield with the helmet and sword of Sparta projects the writing on the wall in stone letters: "Duty, Honor, Country." The Plain is the academy's marching ground where Baron Von Steuben himself drilled his young colonials into shape before the taking of Stony Point. Looking south from the Plain toward the cold gray stone barracks topped by the somber gothic tower of the hilltop chapel, visitors can reflect on the countless young officers who day after day, season through season, gave every hour to earn the right to defend their country. The statues of George Washington, Dwight Eisenhower, Douglas MacArthur, and George Patton guard the entrances to their beloved academy, spread from center to flank and rear guard, as if obeying some mystical tactical scheme created by conjunction of their brilliant military minds. The tough stone buildings bear further names; Grant, Lee, Sherman, and Pershing. In no other place is the raw significance of the reunion of these great names as apparent or important. They came from West Point to lead in the American way, and to West Point they returned, larger than life, an example for the future.

On a promontory over the Hudson to the northwest of the Plain lies the small West Point Cemetery. Amidst centenary trees and playful squirrels lie soldiers from every war America has fought, from unknown privates of the revolutionary war, to members of the special forces killed in action in Southeast Asia. In the peaceful quiet of the West Point hills again the mind wanders to distant battles of the past.

West Point exists to forge America's military leaders and demands a heavy toll of those who dare to rise to the challenge. Every year young hopefuls from across the nation, seventeen to twenty-two years old and of "good moral character," write hopeful letters to the vice president of the United States or to their senators and congressmen for nomination. Also eligible are the sons and daughters of deceased or disabled veterans, former POWs, and servicemen missing in action, as well as children of Medal of Honor winners. Handpicked United States Army members complete the yearly quotas. Once enrolled, the student becomes a part of the 4,400-strong corps of cadets and is assigned to a company. Discipline is strict but fair; the young cadets immediately learn to accept and cherish the academy's sacred honor code which simply states, "a cadet will not lie, cheat, or steal, nor tolerate those who do." The tough first year of breaking in as plebes or freshman cadets by the veteran upperclassmen makes certain the do's and don'ts of the corps are well understood and applied thereafter. Four years of academic training are mixed with military training sessions in which everything from applied sciences, engineering, economics, and foreign languages to airborne, jungle warfare, northern warfare, and ranger training are taught. When a cadet graduates from the U.S. Military Academy with the rank of second lieutenant, he or she is a versatile and well-prepared young officer, ready to assume a position of leadership in the U.S. Army.

Teddy Roosevelt flanked by his Roughriders atop San Juan Hill, Cuba.

West Point likes to state that "much of the history it teaches is made by people it taught." From Jefferson Davis to Norman Schwarzkopf, the list of great Americans who formed with the corps is truly impressive. The Civil War armies led by West Pointers Ulysses S. Grant and Robert E. Lee had officers formed by the academy on both sides of the line in fifty-five of the sixty battles of the war. In each of the other five, there was a West Point graduate on one of the contending sides. Generals George G. Meade, commander of the Army of the Potomac; George H. Thomas, "the Rock of Chickamauga;" Philip H. Sheridan and William Tecumseh Sherman of the Union; and Jonathan T. "Stonewall" Jackson of the Confederate Army — all came from West Point, as did countless other lesser known officers of the war. General John J. Pershing, who led the young AEF to France in the First World War graduated in 1886. Douglas MacArthur, Dwight D. Eisenhower, George S. Patton Jr., Omar N. Bradley, and Henry H. "Hap" Arnold led countless West Point graduates during World War II, while General William C. Westmoreland represented the school in Vietnam. All these men carried in common the pledged allegiance to the code of honor and the fine education of an American officer.

Although army green is the traditional color of the U.S. Army, cadets at West Point wear an elegant uniform of "cadet gray." Approved by the secretary of war in 1816, the academy color was adopted in honor of the gray-clad American army under General Winfield Scott, who defeated British troops in upper Canada two years earlier. The gray rapidly replaced the dark blue of the original uniform introduced by the artillerists and engineers who formed the first classes at West Point. On full dress occasions, the corps of cadets floods the Plain in resplendent gray wool jackets, lined with three rows of brass buttons, and white pants. A black "tarbucket" hat with the golden academy shield and trimmings and black feathers tops the ensemble, made even more striking when worn with the senior year's burgundy cummerbund. Unchanged since its inception in 1816, the impeccable uniform is made at the academy's own tailor shop to specifications more than a century old.

Looking back at the turbulent process of growth and maturing which the United States has undergone in its short history, one fact remains unchallenged; when Americans have gone to battle, they have been led by outstanding military leaders. The country owes that to the United States Military Academy at West Point.

On those few days of celebration when the gray masses of the corps of cadets take a break from their hard work and parade down the Plain with swords and bayonets shining, heads high with resolute steps, the words of General Douglas MacArthur come to life in each and every one of their minds, constantly reminding them of their sacred trust:

> The Long Gray Line
> has never failed us.
> Were you to do so,
> a million ghosts in olive drab,
> in brown khaki, in blue and gray
> would rise from their white crosses
> thundering those magic words:
> Duty, Honor, Country.
>
> — Douglas MacArthur, 1962

The United States Third Infantry

On the third of June 1784, groups of volunteers from the Pennsylvania, New York, New Jersey, and Connecticut state militias, fresh out of the revolutionary war, were brought together to form the First American Regiment, "a body of troops to consist of seven hundred noncommissioned officers and privates properly officered." Commanded by Lieutenant Colonel Harmer, the unit was placed on the volatile frontier which comprised what are today the states of Pennsylvania, Ohio, and Michigan, and where constant conflicts broke out between settlers and the local Indian tribes. The troop was shockingly defeated in their first major campaign against the Miami Indians of Ohio. In response, Congress redesignated it the First Infantry, which would form with several other stronger forces in a concentrated effort to enlarge and strengthen the army. In 1792, just one year after the haphazard beginning, the young soldiers were again beaten by the proud Miamis, forcing another major reorganization. Congress now created the Legion of the United States, and the First Infantry became the First Sub Legion. The command of "Mad Anthony" Wayne, the hero of the daring night attack on Stony Point during the revolutionary war, finally whipped the legion into shape. They began to achieve victories against the Northwest Indians. The decisive battle of Fallen Timbers finally crushed the Miamis, opening most of Ohio for settlement.

From 1798 to 1803, the unit was stationed near modern-day Detroit. A small detachment built the supporting Fort Dearborn, a frontier post at a place the Indians called *Chikago*, "skunk," in their native language. The post would eventually grow into one of America's leading cities. Members of the unit were instrumental in pioneering westward expansion. Both Captain Meriwether Lewis of the Lewis and Clark Expedition — which successfully drove west along the Missouri River, over the Rockies to the Pacific — and First Lieutenant (later General) Zebulon Pike, who moved southwest into Spanish territory, were members of the First in those pioneering days.

Once again, the regiment was redesignated First Infantry of the United States Army, joining with another four sister units in the newly formed force. As war against the British broke once again in 1812, the First Infantry found itself operating on the Canadian border. Initial setbacks were reversed in 1814 as the regiment participated in the first victory for American regulars. Led by General Jacob Brown, the Americans engaged experienced British veterans of the Napoleonic Wars in Spain at the Chippewa River in Ontario, as well as in the fierce encounter at Lundy's Lane.

Leathernecks man a machine gun on the western front. WWI.

One year after the end of the war, the First Infantry was consolidated with the Fifth, Seventeenth, Nineteenth, and Twenty-eighth Infantry regiments. The new numerical designation would follow the position of its commanding officer in the army's seniority system. The commander of the First Infantry was the third-highest ranking colonel, thus gaining the Third Infantry. The Third Infantry has retained its designation to this day and constitutes the oldest regiment in the United States Army.

In 1840, the flamboyant West Pointer Lieutenant Colonel Ethan Allen Hitchcock led the entire unit, 690-strong, as it participated in the Second Seminole War against the fierce Chief Osceola in the Florida Everglades. A bloody guerrilla-style war was further complicated by the swampy terrain. Rigorously trained by Hitchcock, the Third earned a reputation as a highly skilled unit and soon gained the upper hand in the lightning skirmishes against the Seminoles, who were famous for their brutal scalping and torturing of prisoners.

When tempers began to flare over the U.S. annexation of Texas, the Third was poised on the southwestern border with Mexico for the conflict which would perhaps be the most significant in forging the regiment's traditions.

The war opened with a Mexican attack on General Jacob Brown's troops stationed at Fort Texas across the Texas border. Moving to relieve him was a 2,300-man force including the Third Infantry commanded by General Zachary Taylor. On 8 May 1846, the two forces met only ten miles to the northeast of the fort at a place called Palo Alto. Mexican general Mariano Arista had six thousand men under his command and immediately ordered a cavalry charge against the forming Americans. After five hours of thunderous rifle and artillery fire, the Mexicans were pushed back with heavy casualties against only nine American soldiers killed. Moving south toward the besieged fort, General Taylor once again met Arista's men. Rather than risk another all-out attack, Arista had prepared trenches and defensive barricades on a dry river bed facing a ravine called Resaca de la Palma. Taylor immediately deployed his troops and advanced against the waiting Mexicans. Again the superior firepower of the smaller American force won the day. After several hours of tough fighting, the Mexican forces began a retreat across the Rio Grande pursued closely by the American troops. Mexican casualties were high as Taylor's troops picked off fleeing Mexicans crossing the river. Others drowned from exhaustion after the fierce fighting on the Texas side of the border.

Undaunted, Taylor's troops crossed into Mexico ten days later, settling at Matamoros to allow reinforcements and supplies to catch up. On 21 September, his forces found themselves before a large Mexican force firmly occupying defensive positions at the city of Monterrey. The Third Infantry was part of the first wave of attackers to storm the city. Enemy cannons were aimed at important street intersections and snipers fired from windows and openings on every building. Despite incredible losses, the American unit held its ground throughout the night until the ammunition was depleted. Even then it remained under Mexican fire until reinforcements could be brought in from the rear.

In December 1846, the Third Infantry was transferred to General Winfield Scott's army, which would open a second front with the first large-scale landing by the United States Army at Vera

Peasant women struggle along as a medic fights for a young G.I's life in the Italian front. WWII.

Cruz on Mexico's eastern coast. The Third was one of the first units ashore. After marching fifty-five miles (ninety kilometers) inland toward Mexico City, Scott's 8,500 troops came across a large Mexican army of twelve thousand at the mountain pass of Cerro Gordo. Among the positions blocking the way was the fortress of El Telegrafo, which the Third took with a charging uphill bayonet assault. For that gallant action, the unit would eventually be allowed to march with fixed bayonets on official U.S. Army parades.

At Churubusco, another bayonet charge by the Third established the unit's reputation as a hard-hitting, unstoppable force. At the decisive battle of the war where the Mexican army braced for the final defense of the capital, the Third thrust itself toward the top of Chapultepec Hill. Scaling with ladders and pickaxes, moving steadily forward, they bravely captured the heavily defended fortress. According to legend, a member of the Third Infantry's band participated in the final storming of Chapultepec Hill armed only with a drum major's baton. After the Mexican defeat, General Persifor Smith, who commanded the division of regulars to which the Third was attached, presented the regiment with a beautiful baton. The baton was made of wood from the flag pole that stood in the Grand Plaza of Mexico City and of pure Mexican silver. It was carried for many years by the successive band majors of the regiment, finally becoming the oldest and most valued trophy, kept in the regiment's museum in an elegant display.

On 14 September 1847 the Third Infantry led the victorious troops into Mexico City. As the Third passed the general staff of the conquering army, General Scott solemnly stood and said to the assembled officers, "Gentlemen, take off your hats to the Old Guard of the army." From that day, the Third Infantry has become famous worldwide as the Old Guard.

Upon returning to the United States, the Old Guard was stationed on the New Mexico-Texas border and saw much action protecting settlers, guarding mail and supply wagons, and fighting the tough Navajo Indians who ravaged the region.

When the Civil War broke out, the Third was in Texas hastily making preparations to sail toward the front. Ships of the Union navy would pick up the contingent off the Texas coast. Three companies lagged behind and were captured by forming rebel militias, but the bulk of the regiment was able to slip away. On the way to the gulf, the Third had to pass through San Antonio, a beehive of rebel activity where trouble was expected. Arriving at the city's outskirts, the Old Guard formed in parade order and marched in with colors flying, drums roaring, the band playing under the tempo of the drum major's baton, and every soldier pacing ramrod straight, creating the most martial of impressions. The Old Guard passed through San Antonio with no incidents to record.

The Union armies were green at the opening of the conflict, formed mostly of young volunteers from several state militias with practically no military training. With the cream of Washington's society following along in carriages with picnic lunches to see the boys in blue win a battle, the young union troops marched confidently toward their first engagement at Bull Run. What they encountered was far from what they expected. Tough, well-led, and motivated Confederate troops cut into their ranks with incredible ease forcing them back toward the capital just behind the terrified civilians. Only one small unit of battle-hardened veterans placed in skirmish line stood its ground, preventing the defeat from becoming a desperate rout and a rebel walkover through Washington, D.C. The advancing gray lines charged toward them and there they were stopped. The Old Guard had saved the capital on the opening day of the war.

A few days later while forming as part of the provost guard of Washington, the Third was reviewed by President Abraham Lincoln. "There are the men who saved your army at Bull Run," pointed General McDowell. "Yes," replied the president, "I have heard of them."

From that brave beginning, the Old Guard joined nearly every major battle with the Army of the Potomac, earning battle honor after battle honor to finish the war with twelve campaign streamers on the regimental colors.

With the country back to normal, the Third resumed its frontier duties and fought the Comanches in the areas between western Kansas and the Rocky Mountains. They later saw action in both the Spanish-American War and the Philippine Insurrection. In the opening of the twentieth century, a brief two-year period in Alaska presented the Third the opportunity to become one of the first military units ever to be engaged in an ecologically oriented mission: they patrolled the area to prevent the senseless slaughter of the numerous herds of caribou that roamed the region. In 1909 they were again sent to the Philippines to contain the Moro tribesmen from Mindanao, who seemed to consider it a sin not to kill white men.

After World War I, the entire army was greatly reduced. From September to November 1921, for example, First Sergeant Warren Donald was all that was left of Company L. Every evening he would fall in, give himself the proper command, inspect his own uniform, and then report to the CO.

Although the Third saw no formal combat action in World War II as it patrolled the northern tip of Newfoundland, it was posted to Europe, arriving in France just as the guns fell silent, being assigned to Berlin as part of the occupation army. In November 1946 following another post-war reduction of the military, the unit was disbanded. Two years later, it was reactivated and assigned ceremonial duties for being the oldest infantry unit in the U.S. Army. Stationed at Fort Myer and later Fort McNair as well, the Old Guard began the duties which today make it famous throughout the world.

Responsible for the defense of the capital and for all major ceremonial duties performed by the army, the Old Guard has not, however, become purely a parade unit. It was sent to Vietnam where it saw action in the Saigon-Long Binh area. In that theater of war Corporal Michael J. Holland of the second battalion received a posthumous Congressional Medal of Honor for throwing his body over an enemy grenade thus saving his entire squad.

Today the First Battalion (Reinforced) of the Old Guard plays a central role in military ceremonies in the nation's capital, escorting the president, foreign heads of state, and other high-ranking officials; rendering guard over the Tomb of the Unknown Soldier at Arlington National Cemetery; and maintaining age-old traditions of the U.S. Army for the upcoming generations. Subdivided into its various companies, the Third Infantry is prepared to perform each of these duties with the utmost proficiency. The Commander in Chief's Guard, composed of soldiers measuring 6'2" to 6'4" (1.88 to 1.93 meters) form for ceremonies at the White House or in escort duties for the president. The unit was formed in 1971 at the request of then-President Richard Nixon, just back from England and greatly impressed by the drill of the Household Division's Guards at Buckingham Palace.

At the Tomb of the Unknown Soldier, another detachment of the Old Guard keeps watch over the resting grounds of America's military heroes. Throughout the day perfectly poised sentries wearing regulation dark glasses and carrying shiny M-1 Garand rifles kept in mint condition march the regulation twenty-one steps up and then down the passageway before the large marble memorial. As they complete their beat, returning to the initial central position, they stop, immobile for a regulation twenty-one seconds before proceeding on their vigil. Their movements are consistently perfect, almost robotlike. Their stride is all hips and knees, demanding the least physical exertion possible, and ultimately elegant. Their gaze is menacingly cold.

Throughout the day, as the guard changes at the monument, a young noncommissioned officer marches out and proceeds to inspect both incoming and outgoing men without himself losing the slightest poise. The small crowd gathered watches in awe, as without a single word, an unbelievable rifle checking routine takes place before their eyes. Bolts clicking and the dull thud of wood slapping strongly against the men's gloved palms explode through the sudden silence, while shiny Garands twirl and rock through the air, handled by the expert hands of these modern-day gunslingers.

Ike Eisenhower rallies U.S. Airborne troops of the Screaming Eagles on their way to Normandy.

Throughout the short ceremony, not a word is exchanged, no emotion is shown, no body language breaks the perfection of these soldiers' movements.

On Memorial Day weekend, the Third lines up for duty at three in the morning. For national funerals, such as President Kennedy's in 1964, the Old Guard renders the country's final military honors, lining the streets of the capital as a last homage to the nation's greats.

On parades and state occasions the Old Guard is distinguishable by their dark blue uniforms with yellow trimmings. While all other elements of the U.S. Army wear the regulation dress greens, the Old Guard, also known as the Blues, is the only army unit allowed to wear its traditional blue uniforms. Another important distinction is their use of actual medals rather than the regulation ribbons. Each member of the Old Guard is expected to press his own uniform and to strip and shine their own brass to perfection, which they do with immeasurable pride.

The Old Guard uses exact replicas of their first 1784 uniforms as well as the perfect performance of that period's military drill. Following Baron Friedrich Von Steuben's original military manual, the young soldiers clad in Revolutionary uniforms and wigs and carrying .75-caliber brown Bess muzzle-loaders, parade led by their Continental Color Guard in the slow march of the time — arms outstretched and immobile to the side with open, flat-faced fists — wheeling in two ranks of "nine in front six to the rear" to the tune of the traditional drum and fife corps also dressed in Revolutionary garb. Completing the Third Infantry's impressive parade ensemble is the U.S. Army's drill team with their daredevil handling of the M-1 with fixed bayonet and the elegant presence of the U.S. Army band, better known as "Pershing's Own."

Born with the founding fathers and having more than earned the distinction of immortalizing the traditions of the United States Army, the Old Guard epitomizes the quest for perfection of the American soldier.

The United States Marine Corps

World-renowned for its daring strikes from the sea and the rough demeanor of its men, the United States Marine Corps is perhaps the force that best epitomizes America's fighting spirit. The legend of the tough "leathernecks," clad in battle camouflage or in dress blues, has spanned two centuries and spread to every continent and every ocean on the globe. Storming beaches from armored landing craft or helicopter, conducting missions behind the lines, evacuating civilians from embattled areas, holding positions against numerically superior enemies, and maintaining the tradition of always arriving first at the scene of a fight, the Marines have remained one of America's most loved and respected institutions.

In the fall of 1775, with the infant Continental army desperately short of weapons and gunpowder, Congress created two battalions of American marines who immediately set out on their first raid. Commanded by Captain Samuel Nicholas, a thirty-two-year-old Quaker innkeeper from Philadelphia, 234 men boarded eight small ships and headed toward the Bahamas. At 2 P.M. on 3 March 1776 the marines rowed their whaleboats ashore in their first operational landing to take Fort Montagu, a few miles from the City of Nassau. On the following day, Fort Nassau was taken and the British flag replaced by the Stars and Stripes. Throughout the revolu-

Young Marines raise the stars and stripes atop Mount Suribachi. Iwo Jima, WWII.

tionary war, marines fought on U.S. Navy ships, often manning the cannon or firing their muskets from the tops of masts. Landing parties struck at enemy shore positions and boarded enemy warships in the thick of battle, often destroying the ships themselves with grenades expertly thrust into the powder holds. With the daring young John Paul Jones, Continental marines took the war to the enemy, boldly attacking targets off the European coast, beginning a tradition of striking anywhere at anytime.

Upon returning to the U.S. these troops were issued green uniforms with white jackets and leather collars for defense against enemy cutlass strikes to the neck. This uniform gave birth to the nickname of "leathernecks" the marines love. By the end of the war the corps was disbanded along with the Continental navy. By 1798, however, the marines were not only back on duty but were presented with their own marine band which played at Jefferson's presidential inauguration and at every one since.

In 1800, the corps moved from Philadelphia to southeast Washington, D.C., where new marine barracks were constructed on Eighth and I streets. Still in use, the barracks are the oldest continuously occupied public residence in the nation's capital.

In 1801 the Pasha of Tripoli, Yusuf Karamanli, — one of the feared Barbary pirates who for years had ravaged Christian shipping in the Mediterranean — declared war on the United States, prompting President Jefferson to send successive expeditions against the Tripolitan coast. In 1805, rallied by the flamboyant consul of Tunis, William Eaton, to replace the Pasha with his estranged brother Hamet, young twenty-year-old marine lieutenant Presley Neville O'Bannon led a motley force of seven marines, 500 Egyptian and Greek warriors, and 107 camels through 600 miles (965 kilometers) of scorching desert to attack the city of Derna along with a well-coordinated naval bombardment from the sea. Led by O'Bannon and his marines in a valiant bayonet charge, the city was finally taken and the Stars and Stripes were raised for the first time in the eastern hemisphere. Repeated counter attacks by the Pasha's reinforcements were beaten back until Hamet's men finally defeated his brother's troops completely. In gratitude, Hamet gave O'Bannon his beautiful jeweled scimitar which became the model for the "Mameluke sword," proudly carried by today's marine officers.

The War of 1812 saw America hopelessly unprepared to fight Britain's large ocean-going navy. Nevertheless, the fast, well-armed frigates charged into battle and, greatly due to their sharp-shooting marine contingents, soon began amassing victories over British warships. At Lake Champlain, Bladensburg, and New Orleans, the small contingents of marines fought fiercely to oust the invaders from their land, proving yet again the corps' determination and skill in warfare.

War against the rugged Florida Seminoles followed in the swampy terrain of the Everglades. Foreign action against Cuban and Malay pirates kept alive the tradition of quelling brush-fire wars along the world's coastlines. Similarly, an expedition against Liberian slave traders followed before the corps joined General Winfield Scott's landing at Veracruz and the subsequent march toward Mexico City in the 1846-47 Mexican War. During the campaign — after the storming of Chapultepec and the marine domination of the captured seats of government — an anonymous poet penned the "Marine Hymn" sung to the tune of a popular Offenbach operetta, *Genevieve de Brabant*. Thus the famous lines which commemorated Marine Corps bravery "from the halls of Montezuma, to the shores of Tripoli" became one of America's most well known and revered military tunes. The scarlet stripe in the dress blue trouser of the marine gala uniform was added in memory of the dead in that conflict. Present with Commodore Matthew C. Perry on his historic trip to Japan, the marines were instrumental in showing the might of America's military, thus helping convince the Japanese to begin trade relations with the nations of the west.

In 1859, led by Lieutenant Colonel Robert E. Lee, a company of well-armed marines from the marine barracks in Washington stormed the federal arsenal of Harper's Ferry, Virginia, in one of the first hostage-saving operations in the history of America's military. The Civil War divided the corps and, although the majority sided with the Union, a small contingent flocked to the 600-strong Marine Corps of the Confederacy.

In 1898, the marines were again to land on foreign soil, this time at Guantanamo Bay where they fought the campaigns of the Spanish-American War. Two years later, marines dug in along with forces from allied countries in the Legations Quarter of Peking. One after another, fierce attacks by the fanatical Chinese "Boxers" were repulsed in a siege that lasted fifty-five days. The small marine contingent fought alongside members of Britain's Royal Marines, marines of Italy's famous San Marco Battalion, and German naval infantry. On one particular night, Private Daniel Daly, a young marine from Glen Cove, New York, volunteered to guard the American sector of the Tartar City Wall by himself. By the end of the siege, Daly won a medal of honor.

Throughout the twenty-first century, marines would serve in China, adding the slogan "Gung Ho," or "working in harmony," to their very particular vocabulary. Interventions in the Caribbean were commonplace in the early years of our century, with several landings in Nicaragua, Panama, Honduras, the Dominican Republic, Cuba, Mexico, and Haiti. The image of the tall, young marines in their "Smokey Bear" hats was a common sight on every coastline under the influence of America's growing gunboat diplomacy.

In May 1912, First Lieutenant Alfred A. Cunningham took to the air at Annapolis, Maryland, taking the first step for marine aviation, the first pilots seeing almost immediate action in the upcoming world conflict over the skies of Europe.

Although battle-hardened from countless landings and emergencies before the world conflict, the First World War had a special flavor for the U.S. Marine Corps. A golden page of glory for the corps was written at a small place known as Belleau Wood.

In May 1918, the German armies spread across the western front tried a last ditch, all-out offensive to break the trench war stalemate by throwing their elite storm troopers at the Allied lines. The thrust opened with resounding success as French and British troops were swept back toward the gates of Paris. With a rapidly deteriorating situation at hand, the American Second Division was called forward to "button-up" several holes on the line. Among the units composing the Second Division was the Fourth Marine Brigade, made up of the Fifth and Sixth Marine Regiments and the Sixth Machine Gun Battalion.

Placed in a thin, defensive line before the wheat fields that stretched out toward Belleau Wood, the young, untrained marines braced for the inevitable German attack. What little combat experience they had was more than compensated by the traditional marine doctrine of expert sharpshooting. "One well-placed shot" had been the rule since the continental marines atop sail riggings on U.S. ships picked off their British foes one at a time almost 150 years earlier. As the crack German attackers charged forward in tight combat order, they were mowed into the wheat fields by the expertly placed marine rifle and machine gun fire. By late afternoon, the German attack had failed. The marines had held the line. Their French allies, however, were exhausted and pulling back in droves to regroup. Passing through the American lines, a French officer ordered marine Captain Lloyd Williams to withdraw his men to more secure positions in the rear. "Retreat, hell," replied the young leatherneck captain, "We just got here!"

At 5 P.M. on 6 June 1918, the marines, having beaten several German attempts to reach their lines, were poised to attack. As hot German machine gunfire raked the wheat before the American positions, forty-four-year-old First Sergeant Dan Daly, — the same man who had stood alone atop the Peking Wall and who had won a second medal of honor in Haiti — moved toward the open wheat field. Turning back toward his men, he exclaimed, "Come on, you sons-of-bitches! Do you want to live forever?" With a wild cheer the American marines charged forward. Rather than adopt the common massed charge of the time, the marines split up into small fire teams and moved forward, offering less of a target for the German gunners to hit. Upon reaching the edge of the woods, the young Americans rushed from tree to tree, shooting from cover much as their American Indian ancestors had done in their country's past. Casualties nevertheless were high with almost 20 percent of the brigade being wiped out on the first day alone. For twenty days the battle raged fiercely for that very small piece of French real estate. So valiant and hard fighting were the marines that they rapidly earned the German nickname of *teufelshunde*, or "devil dogs," due to the ferocious bull mastiffs encountered by the advancing Germans in the inner court of the Castle of Belleau in the early days of the war. The name stuck with the marines. They are called devil dogs by friend and foe and react with shrill dog yowls in joyous moments. The marines also took up the British bulldog as their almost sacred mascot, a living reminder of the devil dogs of Belleau Wood. On 26 June, at 7 P.M. the long-awaited message finally arrived at headquarters: "Woods now U.S. Marine Corps entirely."

The Germans were swiftly moved back in what was to prove their last offensive before the final Allied push east. Proud marines paraded in Paris to cheerful cries of "*Vive les marines*" and the French government fittingly renamed Belleau Wood the "*Bois de la Brigade de Marine*." Fighting was tough also at Soissons, Saint Mihiel Blanc Mont Ridge, and the Argonne, but the marines held their own skillfully.

After the war, marine contingents continued to land in Caribbean hot spots, protecting the routes to the strategic Panama Canal as well as American interests against local rebels in Cuba, Mexico, Nicaragua, Haiti, and the Dominican Republic. This almost ceaseless period of small-scale combat did much to prepare the marines' amphibious landing capabilities, taught them useful techniques against guerrilla and jungle opponents, and trained the components of the rapidly expanding Marine Air Wings.

When the Japanese attack at Pearl Harbor swept the United States into WWII, the marines were ready for the island-hopping campaign that would pitch them into a seemingly endless struggle against the fierce Japanese in the far-off malarial jungles and atolls of the Pacific.

Throughout the Pacific, marines led the offensive descending the sides of huge transports in droves from rope ladders and nets toward their landing craft. Under intense fire they would steam toward the beachhead where wave after wave would swarm up the sandy beaches while the enemy fired nonstop from the protection of the nearby jungle. Yard by hard-fought yard was captured from the Japanese as the marines consolidated their positions, only to be swarmed by terrifying banzai attacks which had to be beaten off again and again, many times with rifle butt and bayonet.

Small-scale attacks conducted by small groups of highly trained and well-equipped Marine Raiders, led by gung ho Lieutenant Colonel Evans Carlson, initiated a special forces operations mentality in the corps. Marine Raiders were trained to conduct hit-and-run operations on strategic enemy positions, to serve as shock troops in the vanguard of massed landings, or to lay low and organize guerrilla resistance behind enemy lines. They were capable of marching more than fifty miles (eighty kilometers) a day on an empty stomach and of fighting skillfully with nothing more than their trusted BAR and M-1 rifles, Thompson submachine guns, and their much-prized combat knifes such as the K-Bar and the marine stiletto. Special operations conducted by the raiders were as much gung ho as cerebral, exemplified by the special team of Navajo code talkers, handpicked at stateside reservations and never intercepted by Japanese radio experts eavesdropping on marine communications.

Guadalcanal was the first main step in the marine push toward Tokyo, as the men learned to root the tough Japanese defenders from the disease ridden swamps and jungles. In the air, marine pilots threw their inferior fighters valiantly against the Japanese Zeros until better planes could be rushed from the factories to the front. Tough jungles were also encountered in the struggle to isolate Rabaul. At Tarawa, young marines in spotted camouflage utilities stormed the palm tree-fringed atoll in a frontal attack taking unbelievable casualties before finally dislodging the Japanese, who as elsewhere refused to surrender.

Campaigns in Saipan, the Marshalls, and the Marianas followed, before the marines spearheaded the assault on the Philippines, coming ever nearer to the Japanese home islands. At that point the corps came up against the fortified lava island of Iwo Jima, a sulfurous dot on the vast Pacific halfway between the consolidated U.S. air bases in the Marianas and Japan itself. A base was needed as a halfway point for B-29 bombers striking Japan on long-range missions. Iwo Jima, some 670 miles from each, was chosen.

Defending the island were 23,000 well-armed and motivated Imperial Japanese troops led by the brilliant Lieutenant General Tadamichi Kuribayashi, a highly capable strategist who considered his island the "gateway to Japan" itself. Rather than await the inevitable landings on the beach in open, desperate banzai attacks, Kuribayashi feverishly worked against the clock to transform Iwo Jima into a monstrous fortification for which the attacking Americans would have to fight every step of the way.

Iwo Jima is roughly shaped like a tennis racket some five miles by two and one-half miles (eight by four kilometers) at its widest. Dominating the southern tip of the island lies the awesome 550-foot (170 meter) extinct volcano, Mount Suribachi. The central portion of the island consists of continuously flat land while the northern side rises to become the Motoyama Plateau, a natural fortification protected from the sea by ragged cliffs and ravines with hundreds of caves. Artillery emplacements, bunkers, and a complex eleven-mile (eighteen-kilometer) system of tunnels were expertly built inside this amazing solid rock fortress. The landing beaches on the flat southeast of the island consisted of dark and heavy volcanic ash, which caused men to sink to their ankles and vehicles to become helplessly immobilized.

On the morning of Monday, 19 February, the marines landed with small opposition. Almost immediately they began receiving mortar, machine gun, and rifle fire from an enemy they could not see. Foxholes rapidly dug were immediately filled again by the sliding, coarse black ash. For hours on end, the marines on the beach were hopelessly exposed. By nightfall the beach was littered with hundreds of wounded and dead marines. Carcasses of tanks, trucks, and amtracs burned ferociously into the dusk while, from the top of their dominant positions, Japanese artillery rained hot fire at the attackers who had hastily dug in, expecting a nighttime banzai attack that never came.

On the second day a slow pillbox-by-pillbox attack with flame throwers, grenades, and satchel charges took advancing marines some two hundred yards (220 meters) up Mount Suribachi's steep slopes. It took another two days to finally surround the lead-spitting volcano. Out at sea, waves of Kamikaze planes threw themselves upon the fleet while the tough ordeal continued in Iwo Jima. On Friday, patrols moving toward the top of Suribachi began reporting no opposition. Forty men of E Company led by young Lieutenant Harold G. Schrier moved on hands and knees to climb the steep sides of the volcano. Reaching the top unopposed, they found a piece of steel pipe which they used to tie a small American flag brought ashore inside a map case. Six men raised the flag at the top of Mount Suribachi, one, Private Louis Charlo, a native American Crow Indian. Almost immediately, the beachhead erupted in cheering, while bells and sirens could be heard from the ships at sea. From the entire island, the Stars and Stripes could be seen atop Mount Suribachi. But the fighting in Iwo Jima had only started. It would be so bloody in fact that of the six men raising the flag three would be killed and two wounded before the island finally fell silent.

With marines pouring onto the landing beaches, the fighting turned against the heavy fortifications on the Motoyama plateau. Cave after cave and bunker after bunker were cleaned with unbelievable casualties. Fighting wore on for each hill. On one above Nishi Village, forty-three marines were blown up as the Japanese dynamited their underground command post as it was about to fall. Slowly however, the marines succeeded in pushing General Kuribayashi's troops toward the northwestern tip of the island. The island had been taken but "mopping up" operations lasted until May. Iwo Jima had been the most brutal and costly battle for the Marine Corps. Planned for fourteen days, the battle took more than one month to define and left the attackers with roughly 23,000 casualties, one for every Japanese defender. Out of eighty marine medal of honor recipients in WWII, twenty-two were earned in the sands of Iwo Jima. The touching marine memorial at Arlington National Cemetery portrays in giant size the flag raising moment atop Mount Surubachi. At the base of the statue, Admiral Chester W. Nimitz's words about the Iwo Jima landings are carved in gold: "Uncommon valor was a common virtue."

Okinawa, at the doorstep of Japan, was the last island to be taken before the end of the war. As in Iwo Jima, the enemy dug in, forcing a step-by-step approach and huge casualties. As WWII ended, the marines had matured into a powerful force, battle proven and recognized as a capable military elite. They would have a short time to celebrate their hard won victory. With the rumbling of North Korean tanks over the 38th parallel and into their southern neighbor's territory, the marines were once again among the first to fight. Seoul was easily taken and the weak South Korean and American forces were pushed into a rapidly diminishing position in the country's southern tip, the fifty-mile (eighty kilometer) Pusan Perimeter.

On the night of 2 August 1950, the First Provisional Marine Brigade alongside army troops landed in the Port of Pusan to help hold the line. Taking only their packs, ammunition, rations, and rifles, the marines were immediately boarded onto trains and trucks and sent to the front. Supported by arriving marine aircraft providing close air support, they were able to hold back the North Koreans at a place called "No Name Ridge." Simultaneously, U.S. forces commander General Douglas MacArthur was devising a masterplan that would land an entire marine division far behind the North Korean lines and catch the enemy between the two American forces. The west coast port of Inchon was picked as the ideal landing site. On 23 August the aging general decided, "We shall land at Inchon, and I shall crush them!"

The first marine division was prepared for the task. On D-Day, 15 September, 25,000 men with their backs to approaching Typhoon Kezia and facing the dug-in Communist forces ashore, landed at Inchon. The landing was flawless and soon what had started out as imminent defeat turned to victory and the backbone of the North Korean army was rapidly broken by the American, UN, and South Korean troops. Pushed back from the 38th parallel, the North Koreans retreated all the way toward the River Yalu on the Chinese border with UN troops in hot pursuit. Suddenly, as if flooding from a breached dam, thousands of Red Chinese troops swept into Korea. China had joined the fray!

More than three hundred thousand Red Chinese troops swept in from the north. Soon the First Marine Division was trapped at Chosin Reservoir where they faced a freezing winter and exhaustive Chinese human wave attacks. Among the twenty thousand trapped marines was five-time Navy Cross winner Colonel Lewis "Chesty" Puller, a bold cousin of great American general George S. Patton. Undaunted upon assessing his situation, he stated, "Well, this is just great; it means we can shoot in all directions!" And shoot they did. Despite the sub-zero winds, rampant frostbite and harassment from Chinese outnumbering them five to one, General Oliver P. Smith's marines began a fighting sixty-mile (one hundred kilometer), eighteen-day retreat over the mountains to break out of Chosin toward the coast. According to legend, when inquired if his move was a retreat or retirement, an outraged General Smith bluntly replied, "Retreat, hell, we're just attacking in another direction."

Colonel Chesty Puller led the column's rear moving out along with the covering tanks. His jeep, laden with wounded marines, was the last to pull out. Colonel Puller followed on foot. When they arrived at the port city of Hungnam, where they were successfully evacuated by U.S. ships, they had dragged out with them all their equipment, all their dead, and all their wounded. The Korean War ended in a stalemate, with both armies returning to their previous boundaries at the 38th parallel.

In 1962 marine Colonel John Glenn, Jr., captured the imagination of the world by becoming the first American astronaut to orbit the earth. The virtual peace seemingly enjoyed by the world would soon be put to an end as countless cold war confrontations erupted around the planet.

America was caught in the quagmire of Vietnam and the marines fought the war full force. Landing at Da Nang on 8 March 1965, the marines would amass almost one hundred thousand casualties by the war's end eight years later. During the 1968 Tet Offensive, marines crossed the Perfume River to relieve the Imperial City of Hue, Vietnam's ancient capital. Fighting was fierce house-to-house and casualties were high. After almost a month of heavy fighting, the city was finally recaptured. At Khe San on the Laotian border and slightly south of the DMZ, four marine battalions along with army special forces and South Vietnamese troops endured a bloody five-month siege by Viet Cong and NVA forces before the end of the monsoon season allowed relief to be sent. But fighting wore on and finally by July the base was abandoned. When Saigon was evacuated through Operation Frequent Wind, marines were the last to leave, guarding embassy personnel and high-ranking locals in the last helicopters out. The marines protected the embassy perimeter, one of their main missions worldwide, while a total of 530 helicopter sorties evacuated more than six thousand people from a rapidly falling Saigon.

The painful Vietnam experience forced the U.S. military to reassess their situation. In record time the U.S. forces had a new face. Modern, all-volunteer troops, expertly trained and educated, equipped with state of the art weapons, and led by example, had emerged. The marines began acquiring an all around, special operations, fast reaction character that would transform them into a hard-hitting, self-sufficient corps, operational in any type of terrain. Amphibious landing ships capable of launching landing craft from within the hulls while Harrier jump jets and helicopters operate on the upper decks greatly enhanced the quick reaction and special forces capabilities. Back in the traditional marine camps of Parris Island, Lejeune, and Pendleton, weathered drill instructors in dark brown "Smokey Bear" hats still administered the tough, age-old Marine Corps training. Throughout the eighties, marines adapted to their new role, suffering tragic casualties in the suicide bomb attack at their peacekeeping barracks in Beirut, Lebanon, and spearheading Urgent Fury, the invasion of the tiny Caribbean island of Grenada to rescue U.S. medical students trapped by communist insurgents and Cuban regulars. In 1989, marines participated in Operation Just Cause, the invasion of Panama to bring dictator Manuel Noriega to trial for drug running.

In the recent Gulf War however the marines full capabilities finally came to light. Their combined arms capability, constant readiness, and continuous training at their Twenty-Nine Palms Desert Training Center in the California desert made them the first unit ready for combat. Although an all out amphibious landing against Kuwait's highly-defended beaches never took place — the marines at sea served as decoys, distracting large numbers of Iraqi troops and equipment — almost all other missions for which the marines had been trained were carried out.

Marine pilots participated in the nonstop bombing of enemy targets. Enemy shipping was boarded at sea by heavily armed marine parties. House-to-house fighting was conducted brilliantly when small groups of Recon Marines were left behind amidst large contingents of Iraqis at the abandoned town of Khafji. Just before G Day, Major General Mike Myatt, commander of the First Marine Division, ordered two small three-thousand-man sapper units, code-named Task Forces Taro and Grizzly, ahead of the First and Second Marine Divisions poised to attack the awesome barriers of mines, anti-tank traps, fire trenches, and barbed wire belts. The sappers infiltrated enemy territory and worked feverishly during the night, hiding in holes while the sun shined. Slowly they succeeded in opening three lanes in the sand through which their vehicles could pour through. Even before the war erupted, marines in LAVs were engaging Iraqi tanks faring impressively with fluid tactics and tow wire guided missiles. When the first shots rang out opening G Day, the marines had already had two full days of combat against the Iraqis! On G Day, the two marine divisions charged toward their prepared invasion routes and plowed through Iraqi defenses with incredible ease, fanning out once past the danger, and speeding toward Kuwait City. Fighting all along, marine units were the first to enter the Kuwaiti capital, crowning a brilliantly led and executed operation which General Schwarzkopf stated would be "studied for many, many years to come as the way to do it." The United States Marines had matured into America's faithful elite of "a few good men."

RANGER
HONOR GUARD

(Previous spread) The Third Infantry is the army's elite ceremonial unit. (Top left) An NCO checks for grease stains in the impeccable drill at the tomb of the unknown soldier. (Bottom left) The Third Infantry is directly responsible for the nation's capital. (Bottom right) The Gulf War campaign is the most recent of the battle streamers. The Third Infantry is responsible for all the official U.S. state and territorial flags. (This page) In colonial uniform the Third Infantry performs the two-hundred-year-old drill of America's first soldiers. (Facing page) The unit's commanding officer is among the U.S. Army's most decorated men.

(Page 134) "Semper Fidelis!" The marines are America's most visible elite troops. Tradition is carried out in the flawless manner of the corps. Men of Marine Barracks Washington march out onto the turf at the Iwo Jima Memorial. This is the only place where white trousers are worn with the dress blues. (Page 135) Marines devote painstaking time to their uniforms. Masking tape is used to bind together clothing underneath the perfectly pressed blue blouse. Once dressed up, marines never sit down until the ceremonies are over.

U.S.
U.S.
HONOR GUARD

UNCOMMON VALOR WAS A COMMON VIRTUE

(Facing Page) Drum Major, United States marine Drum and Bugle Corps. A full United States Marine Band, once commanded by John Philip Sousa — one of America's foremost musicians — is known as the President's Own as it played for the president since Jefferson's inauguration. The Drum and Bugle Corps is a smaller marching unit that combines great music with perfect drill. Once President Eisenhower, an army man, joked to the marine commandant that the U.S. Marine Band was in fact his, not the commandant's, who without losing a beat replied that he did not mind that, because he had the Drum and Bugle Corps. The story stuck, and the unit is today "the commandant's own." (This page top left) Marines have pride in their corps. (Top Right) A young marine brings out Lance Corporal Chesty X, the marine mascot. (Center left) The marine insignia derives from that of the Royal Marines who also sport the globe and anchor, although with the eastern hemisphere depicted rather than the western. (Bottom) Impeccable. The marines.

USMC
MB
WASH DC
A

- Sporting their everyday "Charlie" uniforms, marines practice their drill to perfection. At "Eight and Eye" as Washington Marine Barracks are affectionately called, the marines march in the exquisite "Slide and Glide" manner, also called by some "the snake walk," a move which would seem almost ladylike were it not performed by hundreds of tough M-1 Garand toting marines. Among the several attractions provided by Washington's marines is the Silent Drill Team, a twenty-four-man rifle platoon which performs precision drill and death defying moves with rifle and bayonet without verbal commands. The effect is electrifying.

During the Revolutionary War, George Washington called West Point The Key to America, such was the fortress' strategic value. It was the scene of a daring attempt at treason when Benedict Arnold successfully severed the giant chains that prevented the British fleet from sailing up the Hudson. Luckily, the local troops got ahold of the situation in time. West Point has since become the spawning ground for America's military leaders. The Army mule(Top Left) is a much revered mascot always present on parade and in football. (Top Right)The Academy crest. (Center)Great Americans are buried in West Point's quiet cemetery. (Bottom Left)Cadets flood The Plain.

Viewed from The Plain, West Point evokes countless acts of American bravery. (Left)Color Guard. West Point's grey, yellow and black stem from the three colors of the components of gunpowder. (Page 142)Tar Bucket toss on graduation day.These young men and women are now ready to lead. (Page 143) Legend has it that General George S.Patton as a cadet, did his utmost to stay away from the Academy library. Ironically, that is the building his statue faces today!

CANADA

Riders of the Red Serge

The Royal Canadian Mounted Police

The Foot Guards

The Royal Canadian Mounted Police are one of the most recognized symbols of Canada, second only to the flag. Elegant in the full dress Red Serge, light brown Stetson with its characteristic folds on the crown, Sam Browne holster belt, and Strathcona riding boots and spurs, the Mountie is a living symbol of Canada's nation-building struggle. On their regulation sixteen-hand-high thoroughbreds they spark the imagination of Canadians and foreigners alike. Their nationwide presentations of the Musical Ride are a spectacular demonstration of riding proficiency, as handpicked constables and stallions perform beautifully choreographed moves. Since recruit equitation practice was discontinued in 1966, the Musical Ride is the last opportunity one has to see the RCMP on horseback with Red Serge and lance. Today's Mounties, driving modern patrol cars or flying helicopters equipped with forward-looking infrared-TV monitors, are proud members of what may well be the best police force in the world.

The Canadian Armed Forces, highly professional and battle hardened, also maintain a strong link to their old ways and scarlet tunics. British traditions are maintained in Canada. To see the precision drill of the Foot Guards at Parliament Hill is comparable to watching their magnificent brothers at Buckingham Palace similarly clad in bearskin hats and scarlet tunics. The Parliament Foot Guards and the Royal Canadian Mounted Police each embody the fighting traditions of many years of hard-won battle honors.

After turbulent years of violent struggle between the French, English, Americans, and the native Indians, Canada finally remained in British hands. In 1867, however, confederation was granted and British troops left the huge wilderness in the hands of the native Canadians.

Since the late 1600s all of western Canada, Oregon, and Washington had been controlled by the Hudson's Bay Company, a commercial enterprise specializing primarily in fur-trading with the native people. Upon receiving dominion status, state control over such vast territory became necessary, and the fledgling Canadian government set out to establish its presence in the vast western prairies.

Almost immediately a rebellion broke out at Red River in present day Alberta when whiskey traders moved in to claim the void left behind by the British trading establishments. The local Indians were being decimated in growing numbers as the traders adulterated the whiskey to strengthen its effects and increase their profits. One recipe of the time even included chewing tobacco, red pepper, Jamaica Ginger, molasses, and red ink added to the spirit, creating a potent concoction of dubious effects.

Most of the rough traders and trappers of the region were local *Metis*, half-bloods of French and Indian stock led by Louis Riel. Riel established a provisional government and tried to come to terms with the Canadian authorities. The government treated this act as a rebellion. The newly created militia of the Quebec and Ontario Rifles and the Second Battalion of the Sixtieth King's Royal Rifle Corps quickly despatched an expedition. The rebellion collapsed with little loss of life and Riel fled south across the border. A small mounted police force left behind at Fort Garry was the first organized police force in Canada's western territory. The whiskey traders were forced further west. Soon after, the recent massacre of a band of Assiniboine Indians by white traders in the Cypress Hills was resolved and the perpetrators were prosecuted. The Canadian government was slowly making its presence felt.

Aware of the problems afflicting her southern neighbors move westward, Canada decided to forestall the possible unrest in her own western expanses by creating an effective military force, capable of ensuring law and order as well as Canadian sovereignty. On 23 May, a bill was passed creating the Northwest Mounted Police, forefather of today's mounted police.

In September 1873, Lt. Col. George French, the newly appointed commissioner of the force, decided to move a large contingent west to the junction of the Bow and Belly rivers where Fort Whoop-up, the whiskey trader's base, was reputed to be. In the heat of July 1874, after detailed planning and preparations, the force was ready for the Great March West. The long columns of wagons, carts, mobile kitchens, field guns, and even herds of cattle providing the beef ration moved along at an average twenty-six miles a day. The heat of summer had dried the rough prairie grass and not a day went by when horse and oxen would not die on the trail. Much of the territory through which the force passed was unknown Blackfoot land and a force of lancers in scarlet tunics was handpicked to impress the Indians. Seventy-two days and 1,009 miles (1625 kilometers) later, the force reached its final destination.

The men composing the Great March West were recruited mostly from eastern Canada and brought along their mid-Victorian values. The officers, mostly men born in the United Kingdom, had a very different outlook from the settlers who created the Wild West south of the border. On leaving the force, these men were given land grants to encourage them to settle the West. They in turn influenced the development of their communities.

The NWMP soon established control over the prairies. In many small communities, the men of the force combined the duties of policemen with those of judge, jailer, marriage counselor, and any other office necessary at the time. The high level of training of the officers prevented any type of police tyranny. The force was soon

Capt. John French and other members in the first uniform of the force.

A group of officers outside of Dawson Detachment, July 1900.

welcome throughout the prairies. The local Indians were respected and protected by the men of the NWMP. According to the words of Crowfoot, chief of the Blackfoot, as he accepted the Blackfoot Treaty in 1877: "If the police had not come to this country, where would my people be today? Traders and whiskey were killing us in growing numbers. The Mounted Police have protected us as a bird's feathers protect it from the frosts of winter."

The Metis had been routed but not defeated. In 1885 a Metis rebellion broke out with guerrilla-style attacks devised from their experience on the buffalo hunt. A trading post at Duck Lake was taken and an ambush killed twelve policemen of the first force dispatched. A larger force eventually subdued the Metis. Louis Riel, who had been recalled from exile to lead the rebels, was captured, tried, and hanged for treason.

As the development of the West increased, so did the NWMP's forewarnings of Indian unrest caused by the rapidly diminishing buffalo herds, which determined the basis of their nomadic life. With the coming of the railway, settlement increased tenfold. The protection of the Indians in reservations became one of the priority NWMP missions.

In the United States, the Sioux and Cheyenne defeated Gen. George A. Custer's Seventh Cavalry at Little Bighorn. The U.S. Army immediately launched a firm campaign against the Indian tribes, and the Sioux, led by Sitting Bull, fled across the border into Canada. Canada was justly concerned about the sudden appearance of a warlike Indian nation with ancestral animosity to some of the local Indian tribes. Unwilling to risk damaging diplomatic relations with the United States, the NWMP entered negotiations with the Sioux while providing food and shelter to Sitting Bull's tribes. Eventually a peaceful arrangement was met and the Sioux returned across the border and signed a peace treaty with the U.S. government at Fort Buford, North Dakota.

In 1894, the NWMP began patrolling the Yukon region adjacent to Alaska where newly found gold sparked an enormous influx of fortune seekers. In an attempt to secure law and order in such a volatile environment, the Mounties mediated gambling, prostitution, the granting of liquor licenses, and major disputes wherever necessary. As in the plains, these duties were carried out with fairness and integrity. The force soon held control of the region. One constable was generally enough to control a large area, and the NWMP legend grew rapidly.

In 1897 the NWMP was invited to parade in Queen Victoria's Diamond Jubilee and caused quite a stir in London when they appeared in Stetsons, prairie dress, and crossed bandoliers. By 1890, the NWMP was already patrolling the arctic regions in Canada's far north due to growing activities by traders and whalers. A patrol network on dog teams was set up, rapidly controlling the area and establishing good relations with the local Inuit tribes.

In the last year of the eighteenth century, Canada was called upon to provide manpower for Great Britain's struggles against the elusive South African Boer Commandos. Initially surprised on the battlefield by Boer hit-and-run tactics, spectacular horsemanship, and accurate marksmanship, the British reacted by recruiting similarly proficient outdoorsmen from among their Canadian, Australian, and New Zealand brothers. Britain asked for volunteers and young Canadians responded in droves. These men were hardy and adventuresome, still possessing the initiative and spirit of life on the frontier.

A first 1,000-man contingent of the Royal Canadian Rifles left for South Africa in early 1900. They were eventually joined by more troops and formed the Canadian Mounted Rifles. On 18 February they made their first strike at Paardenberg Drift. On the twenty-seventh, the Boer's commemorated Majuba Day, the nineteenth anniversary of their victory at the Battle of Majuba. The British launched a large-scale attack against the trenches at Paardenberg, intending to make it a day of revenge rather than celebration. A bloody battle was fought in which thirty-four Canadians died and more than one hundred were wounded.

After an initial frontal attack by the Canadian troops was met by a hail of gunfire, several wounded men lay in no-man's land while a second assault was being prepared. Well-placed Boer snipers peeked out of their trenches, awaiting any foolhardy move to raise the casualty count. Having located a wounded comrade by his desperate moans, stretcher-bearer Richard Thompson jumped over the top of his trench, placed his pipe in his mouth, and calmly walked over to where the wounded man lay while the astounded Boer defenders looked on in awe. Thompson was awarded one of the five "Queen's Scarves of Honor," handknit by the queen herself for the noblest men in the conflict. The Canadians carried the day at Paardenberg and were instrumental in routing out General Cronje's army in this major British victory of the war. Canadian troops had been bloodied overseas for the first time. Fourteen years later, more blood would be spilled in the desperate fighting on the western front.

RCMP in furs against the rough Canadian winters.

Canadian troops go "Over the Top" at the Somme.

World War I began on 4 August 1914 with the German invasion of Belgium. On 6 August, the Canadian prime minister's offer of troops was accepted and the Canadian Expeditionary Force was immediately assembled. In April 1915, the Canadian trenches at Ypres were flooded with a new weapon, poison gas. After a short bombardment, the Germans released more than 160 tons of chlorine gas against the Canadian division. More than 6,000 casualties were reported. In 1916, Canadian forces distinguished themselves at the Somme offensive, although the cost was high. More than 24,000 were dead, wounded, or missing after three months of slaughter in northeast France.

The year 1917 found the Canadians poised to assault Vimy Ridge on the Arras offensive. This hillock, long considered impregnable, was successfully assaulted by a thoroughly planned combined arms assault. Enemy artillery was neutralized by the then new concept of counterbattery fire using aerial photos and observation as well as sound ranging. Undetected, special units dug miles of tunnels and caverns that extended throughout the front lines, allowing the heavily laden infantry to begin their attacks almost on top of the enemy's forward trenches. On 9 April 1917, under driving sleet and snow, the four Canadian divisions finally went "over the top" in full strength and overran the German positions without much difficulty, a brilliantly led and executed campaign in a war of few decisive victories. The Canadian victory at Vimy Ridge, in fact, was analyzed by a special study group from the French army impressed by the punch and swiftness of the assault. In 1917 the Canadians were also involved at Passchendaele, or Second Ypres, where they lost 16,000 troops in the killing fields.

In the last year of the war, the Canadian forces fought in the tip of the Allied spear, assaulting the Hindenburg fortifications, breaching the Canal du Nord, and taking Cambrai and the infamous Bourlon Woods. More than 600,000 Canadians, out of a population of 8,000,000, saw service in WWI. More than 60,000 lost their lives in the quagmire of the western front.

During the 1920s and 1930s, the now Royal Canadian Mounted Police continued patrolling the far reaches of the country. The prefix Royal was granted in 1904 by King Edward VII for gallant services during the Boer War. In 1920, as a result of the reorganization of the Federal Police Forces, the Royal Northwest Mounted Police absorbed the Dominion Police to become the Royal Canadian Mounted Police, Canada's federal law enforcement and security agency as we know it today. In the Yukon in 1932, it hunted down the elusive "Mad Trapper," Albert Johnson, who had killed a Mountie and wounded another when they checked complaints that he had been tampering with Indian trap lines. A master of evasion, Johnson had the habit of moving backwards through the snow-covered woods, presenting footprints in the opposite direction. He was nevertheless hunted and finally surrounded and captured by RCMP troops and aircraft. Around the same time, a Fort Benton headline stated, "these Mounties seem to fetch their man every time," from which a legend was gradually woven. The force was also involved in the hunt for both fascist and communist sympathizers and spies, a duty it would perform meticulously until substituted by the Canadian Security Intelligence Service in 1984.

With the outbreak of World War II, Canadians again braced for a worldwide conflict. Although a large number of troops were sent to England as reserves, the first Canadian troops to see combat were the Royal Canadian Rifles and the Winnipeg Grenadiers, sent to Hong Kong to supplement British defenses against the Japanese onslaught. They had scarcely arrived when the Japanese attacked, overrunning the island one day after the surprise attack at Pearl Harbor.

In Europe the Second Canadian Infantry Division was selected to conduct a full-scale landing at the French port of Dieppe. Under cover of darkness and strict radio silence, the small task force carrying some 6,000 Canadian troops steamed resolutely toward the French Coast. Unfortunately, the left flank of the convoy came across a small German naval force and the alarm was sounded.

Alerted by their naval pickets, the German shore defenses reacted with furious fire, catching the Canadian troops in deadly cross fire as they landed on the pebble beaches of Dieppe. A little more than one-third of the troops made it back to England. The rest lay dead or were captured.

In July 1943 the Canadians once again struck against Europe, this time at Pachino in southern Sicily. They proceeded up the boot of Italy alongside the Allied advance. The Battle of Monte Cassino, one of the bloodiest of the Italian campaign, involved massive use of Canadian troops who valiantly engaged crack German paratroop forces in the ruins and mountain crags that led to the hilltop monastery. There were more than 25,000 Canadian casualties throughout the Italian campaign.

In northern Europe, the Canadian army landed at Juno Beach during D-Day and pushed inland, driving the Wehrmacht out of Caen. It then advanced to the low countries, liberating Antwerp and several Dutch cities before joining the violent battle for the Rhineland. A total of 45,000 Canadians lost their lives in WWII, a terrible price to pay for victory. After WWII and the creation of the United Nations, it was Canadian Prime Minister Lester B. Pearson, who envisaged the formation of the United Nations Peace-keeping Force, the Blue Berets. Since the first mission of UN troops in Korea, Canada has participated in every UN mission. Including operations in Iraq during Desert Storm, more than 85,000 Canadians have worn the blue beret of the United Nations.

Throughout the years, Canadians have come a long way from conquering their vast wilderness to policing the world's trouble spots.

(Facing) A recent poll found that the image of the Mountie is the second most well-known Canadian icon after the flag. Marching proud, the band evolved in large strides from the first notes sounded during the Great March West when fifes were accompanied by a large tin dish thumped with tent pegs. (Above left) The service weapon is the .38-mm Model 10 Smith & Wesson revolver. (Above right) Bugler in Red Serge. Unfortunately, this uniform is no longer worn "on the beat," only on ceremonial occasions and on the world famous Musical Ride. (Left) Ceremonial mace and battle honors are carried by the drum major.

The Royal Canadian Mounted Police is presently composed of more than 18,000 members and equipped with more than 6,000 transport vehicles including twenty-nine aircraft, a large variety of boats, and more than fifty horses. Modern day Mounties are engaged in all aspects of police work from traffic control to narcotics, terrorist suppression roles, investigation, and even computer crime. Known by their bilingual title the RCMP/GRC (Royal Canadian Mounted Police/Garde Royale du Canada), the Mounties are perhaps the most well-trained police force in the world. (Above) Mantiens le Droit, "Maintain the Rights."

RCMP GRC
POLICE
RCMP GRC
POLICE

Canada's Foot Guards parade on a clear summer day in Ottawa. Their uniforms and traditions are almost exactly the same as those of their British counterparts.Note however the maple leaf insignia on shoulder boards as well as their US made M16 Rifles.

In Almohade times, whole armies would assemble within the fortified walls of Ribat el Fath (the Camp of Conquest) in preparation for expeditions to Spain. Today, the ramparts still encircle the city of Rabat, Morocco's royal capital. (facing) Although fully combat trained, the Garde Royal is the keeper of Berber and Arabic traditions. The Genur Halberdiers are the Royal Keepers and are always at hand in the presence of a king or a prince.

Morocco's Garde Royal is truly one of the most striking ceremonial units anywhere. (Previous spread) On King Hassan II's birthday, the guards parade through the streets of Rabat at sunset, carrying intricately designed torches which symbolize Aladdin's lamp, the spiritual center of the Arab world. (This spread) Clad in red winter dress, the Garde Royal carry old Moroccan ceremonial rifles, all in perfect firing condition.

that Portugal was almost bankrupted. Alcazarquivir, or the Battle of the Three Kings, was a complete disaster.

Almost four hundred years later, another peninsular army met disaster in Morocco. A Spanish force of 12,000 men led by Gen. Fernando Silvestre set out to find and annihilate the Berber chieftain Abd el Krim, whose name is still legendary in Morocco. Abd el Krim had led the Riff Berbers from the mountains of northern Morocco and established an independent republic in The Riff with an education program, a state bank, and much of the administrative infrastructure of a modern nation. On 21 July 1921 the Berber armies defeated the Spanish troops at the Battle of Anual. Despite the magnanimous size of the French colonial government, Abd el Krim set out to defeat the French as well and rid Morocco of its two colonial rulers. Spain and France, however, put their North African rivalries aside and formed a joint expeditionary force to oust the rebel leader from their colonies. This force, composed mainly of French and Spanish foreign legion troops, landed at Alhucemas Bay on Morocco's Mediterranean coast and moved south to push Abd el Krim's forces against a strong French army advancing northward. After fierce resistance Abd el Krim was forced to surrender, and the French and Spanish colonial boundaries were reinstated. The dream of a free Morocco would have to wait.

The French, in Morocco since the beginning of the century, used North African and foreign legion troops not only to curb rebellion but also to promote economic and social development: building roads, planting crops, creating markets, and administering medical services. Throughout the 1930s and 1940s Morocco remained a peaceful French bastion in North Africa. In the Civil War, North African troops joined Spanish general Francisco Franco's nationalist troops from Ceuta to the Spanish mainland, and Moroccan goums fought bravely alongside the French during World War II, particularly at Monte Cassino on the Italian front. Allied troops landed in Morocco for Operation Torch, eliminating Vichy French forces in North Africa and providing the anvil against which General Montgomery's Eighth Army would hammer the Afrika Korps.

During the 1950s, a lopsided, colonial bureaucracy ensured that Moroccans were given only the most menial of jobs. Rules were so stringent that even the profession of snake charmer was regulated. Finally the winds of change became too fierce to quell. When the popular sultan Mohammed Ben Youssef was exiled by French authorities in 1953, full-scale urban terrorism and rural guerrilla raids began in earnest across Morocco. Extremist French settlers reacted by starting a terrorism campaign of their own. In November 1955 the sultan was brought back from exile in Madagascar to a hero's welcome and in the following year was granted the throne of an independent Morocco as King Mohammed V. Upon his death in 1961, the king was followed by his son, King Hassan II, the current ruler of Morocco.

Challenged throughout his reign, the king has slowly turned Morocco into the most modern and moderate of Muslim nations. In 1963, a brief but bloody desert war was waged against Algeria in a far-lying desert oasis. Morocco stood firm and eventual diplomacy brought a negotiated settlement to the dispute. The 1970s brought a period of dissent in the armed forces. On 10 July 1971 the king's forty-second birthday ceremony was interrupted by 1,400 machine-gun-toting extremist NCO cadets, who gunned down more than one hundred royal guests in a bloody massacre. The king barely escaped, hiding in a bathroom in a corner of the palace. In August of the same year, rebel pilots flying stolen Moroccan Air Force F 5E Tiger aircraft attacked the royal airliner on the king's return from a trip to France. After a series of passes, King Hassan was able to trick the attackers. In a clever move, he grabbed the radio and disguising his voice announced "the tyrant is dead." The jet fighters called off the attack, giving Royalist troops enough time to stamp out the rebellion.

A long-standing dispute with Spain over the Spanish Sahara prompted King Hassan to organize what became one of the most brilliant coups de main ever seen in world diplomacy. The World Court was given the task of deciding who held sovereignty over the vast Saharan territories. Meanwhile, Morocco, awaiting a referendum by local inhabitants, quickly prepared what became known as the Green March. More than 350,000 unarmed Moroccan men and women marched south across the border on 6 November 1975 waving the national flag and copies of the Koran. They camped for three days under the guns of the Spanish foreign legion, and then withdrew when the king announced that the mission had been successful. On 14 November, Spain transferred the administration of the territories to Morocco and Mauritania.

Unfortunately, the victory gained without bloodshed ended when Algerian-backed left-wing Polisario Front guerrillas, fighting for independence in the western Sahara, began a series of armed raids against Moroccan and Mauritanian interests in the region. Ten years of war brought unprecedented political unity in Morocco. In 1981 the Moroccan army reached the turning point of the conflict when it built a vast complex of sand ramparts studded with electronic sensors and machine gun nests extending more than 1,000 miles on the Algerian and Mauritanian borders to deny freedom of movement to the hit-and-run guerrillas. The army thus gained four-fifths of the territory and dragged the conflict into stalemate. In May 1988 Morocco and the Polisario began talks under international mediation.

The people of the Maghreb have succeeded in defending their land against a multitude of invaders, proving that they are ready to back their desire for peace through bravery in war. The Moroccan army has developed into a modern combat force that represents and embodies both Berber and Arab traditions. The Garde Royal, whose mission is the protection of the sovereign as well as the perpetuation of the military traditions of the Maghreb, is based alongside the Royal Palace in Rabat and is formed from handpicked members of Morocco's army. Red or white uniformed guards take up duty at the palace as well as at King Mohammed V's mausoleum, where they are joined by the sober Genur Halberdiers, whose presence is mandatory wherever a king or a prince may be. These elite Berber guards form the exclusive royal bodyguard and, although armed only with the halberd, are trained in diverse military skills.

Sometimes known as the Red Guard, since even the regiment's lorries are painted red rather than army green, the Garde Royal forms a distinctive mix of infantry, cavalry, and music sections. The cavalrymen, reminiscent of Moroccan desert warriors, wear a red *burnoose,* or desert cape, and ride splendid Arab stallions. The infantry, equipped with old ceremonial Moroccan rifles or with trustworthy 7.62-mm FN FALs, drill to perfection, driven by their dedication to the sovereign and to the supreme command of *H'zam,* an Arabic notion comprising a serious, serene, and alert demeanor. The Garde Royal of Morocco is one of the most outstanding elite regiments in the world today.

MOROCCO
Guardians of the Maghreb
The Royal Guard

The Romans dominated Carthage for more than four centuries but never succeeded in conquering the ferocious Berber tribes of the Maghreb el Aska, the "Farthest West" of the Arab world. The "barbarians" blocked every attempt by the Romans to push inland, harassing any man daring to venture into their territory. When 15,000 Vandals invaded North Africa in AD 429, ending Roman rule, the Berber tribes remained unbeaten and proud.

In approximately AD 650, Muslim conquerors decided that the Maghreb's infidels should be converted to Islam. According to legend, the first Arab army to attempt the mission, led by Sidi Okba ibn Nafi, met a Berber army at the Souss valley near Taroudant so large that "Allah alone could count them." Nonetheless, Sidi Okba concluded a series of swift victories, coming at last upon the ocean at the large horseshoe-shaped bay at Agadir. Galloping at full speed, he plunged his stallion into the waves and cried out "Allah! Were it not for this sea, I would ride into distant lands to Doul Karnein [where the sun sets] fighting for your faith and slaying all those who did not believe in you!" After numerous campaigns, Sidi Okba's successor, Hassan ibn an Nu'uman, finally defeated the Berbers by shrewd diplomacy as much as by armed force.

The Berbers embraced Islam with such vigor that they soon formed the bulk of the Arab army. Berber chieftain Tariq ibn Ziad led the army across the straits into Europe to clash against Visigothic Spain. With mostly loin-cloth-clad light infantrymen fighting at the River Lakka (Guadalete), Tariq defeated the Visigoths in AD 711, paving the way for the Muslim conquest of Andalusia. For seven centuries, Spain experienced Arab enlightenment, while the rest of Europe was plunged into the Dark Ages.

The Iberian Peninsula, rich with horses, attracted the Berber armies from across the strait. Arab armies had long realized the importance of the horse in combat. In Mohammed's first armies, horses were led unridden to the battlefield and mounted only for combat itself. Soon, the Arab armies possessed what many would argue is the finest cavalry mount in the world, the Syrian-Arab crossbreed. This horse combined the endurance of the small North African Barb with the heavier Iranian horse's size and power.

As the Arabs encroached on Spain, the Almoravids, a fundamentalist Islamic sect, appeared in the western Sahara. The Almoravid empire flourished for almost two centuries, making its presence felt in the Maghreb as well as in Andalusia. In 1082 the Almoravids ruled a vast portion of North Africa from Ghana to Algiers. In 1085 the Muslims of Andalusia asked the Almoravids to aid them in their struggles after the fall of Toledo to the Spanish kings. The Almoravid armies, initially composed of infantry and a few war camels, soon acquired the ways of their Iberian foes, creating cavalry and organizing their attacks with rallying flags. They spread great fear in the battlefield with the roar of their African war drums. Their massive corps of camels terrified their enemy's horses.

The most striking feature of the Almoravid warriors was their use of the *litham* or face veil. To the Almoravids the mouth was unclean, and unveiled people were known as the "fly-mouthed ones." The high number of black Africans recruited from Senegal on the southern frontier of the empire added to the panic in the Spanish ranks, as did the use of exotic weapons such as the unfamiliar bows and arrows, the huge leather *adarga* shields, and bamboo spears. The Almoravids were also fond of head-hunting, a custom soon emulated by their Christian foes. War trophies such as war flags were collected by both sides, although church bells were clearly an Arab preference and were converted into mosque lamps. Muslims also relied upon surprise attacks, generally avoiding the enemy when he was on foot and ready, preferring to raid those mounted and on the march. In 1086, Yusuf ibn Tashfin, the second Almoravid leader, gained the upper hand against Castille and Leon's forces at the Battle of Zallaka, decisively seizing all of Andalusia from Christian hands. Total peace, however, never came to Muslim Iberia, as the Christians entrenched in the north of the peninsula fought on against the Muslim invader.

Around 1120 the Almohades, a Berber reformist sect from the mountains and cities of Morocco, began pushing the Almoravid forces back, gradually taking all of Morocco and Spain. Coming from an urban background, unlike the Almoravids who were desert nomads, the Almohades set up well-organized, innovative armies against which the Almoravid tactics were no match. The Almohade warriors would form into squares protected by a lance phalanx with slingers and archers inside. The cavalry remained within the squares, leaving to pursue the enemy and returning when threatened. The Almohade warriors customarily shaved their heads before battle and rallied to the call of large green and gold drums whose roar would confuse and frighten the enemy.

The Moors ruled most of southern Spain until the fall of Granada in 1492 to King Ferdinand V and Queen Isabella I of Castile and Aragon. With the last bastion of Moorish resistance overrun, the Christian rulers sought revenge after seven hundred years of Arab domination. Sporadic raids on Christian shipping by North African pirates provided the excuse needed for Spanish and Portuguese kings to organize armed expeditions to the Moroccan coast. These were dark days for Morocco. Christian intolerance led to a renaissance of sorts, as a spirit of *jihad,* or holy war, flourished in the sixteenth century.

In 1541, the Portuguese were routed from Agadir and forced to abandon the ports of Safi and Azemour. These reverses led twenty-four-year-old King Sebastian to seek revenge by launching a crusade against the "barbarians," although advised against such a move by his mostly Jesuit counselors. Sebastian was joined by one of the Saadian kings, Mohammed el Mutawakkil, who had lost his throne to his brother Abd el Malik and was forced to flee to Spain. The cream of Portuguese nobility, blinded by apparent chaos in Morocco, embarked wholeheartedly on their holy foray, landing in Tangiers and Asilah. The 25,000 troops rode inland with the intent of liberating as much territory as possible. Lugging thirty-six bronze cannons, their progress was slowed to a snail's pace, which allowed Abd el Malik to muster a force of 50,000 cavalry. The two armies met at Ksar El Kebir (Alcazarquivir) on 4 May 1578. A rising tide trapped the Portuguese in a fork between the Loukos and Oued el Makhazin rivers. They were massacred by successive Moroccan cavalry charges. King Sebastian and Mohammed drowned in the ensuing confusion. The sultan Abd el Malik died of sickness before the battle was over. Eight thousand Portuguese troops were killed and almost 15,000 captured and ransomed for such a huge amount

Guarding King Mohammed V's mausoleum is one of the guards' main duties. "God's throne is on his horse's back," according to an old Moroccan saying. (Facing) The Garde Royal is supplied with perfectly bred horses of Arab stock. Each of the three cavalry sections rides a different color horse, bay, sorrels, and tans. Note the distinctive Moroccan saddle.

ITALY

Legions of the Peninsula
The Bersaglieri
The Alpini
The Granatieri di Sardegna
Lancieri di Montebello
Corazzieri of the Carabinieri Corps

Few countries place the same importance on military tradition as Italy. In 1861 Guiseppe Garibaldi's "Thousand Red Shirts" advanced from the south and, with Prime Minister Cammillo Cavour of Piedmont and French emperor Napoleon III, defeated the Austrians in the north. The victory brought Italy its independence and paved the way for a constitutionally chosen kingdom of Italy, ruled by the king of Sardinia, Victorio Emmanuelle II. Italy has since created several elite units that still parade their colorful traditions through the streets of this lively country.

Before the twentieth century, the kingdoms of the Risorgimento, and the powerful city-states of the Renaissance, Italy was the seat of the powerful Roman Empire.
For almost eight centuries, the mighty Roman legions swept throughout Europe and North Africa, displaying an invincible combination of tactics and training that are admired to this day. The legions were formed mostly of a compact mass of infantry divided into hundred-man centuries. A dependable officer, or centurion, would be responsible for all aspects of training, drill, logistics, and actual combat in his century. Auxiliary troops composed of archers, slingers, and light cavalry operated in the flanks or as skirmishers and had little impact on the final results of battle.

Legion tactics were simple. Centurions would rally their troops before battle, stiffening their spirit by reminding the men of the horrors of capture if their enemies were barbarians. Legionnaires were armed with the *pilum*, a lance-like weapon made of a four-foot wooden shaft attached to a three-foot iron spike with a tempered tip but a soft body. This allowed the pila to penetrate wooden shields with ease but would make them very hard to extract, thus destroying the enemy's protection against small arms. The legion advanced line-abreast against the enemy, threw their pila, and rapidly closed to within arm's length where they could hack through the exposed enemy with their short swords.

Legionnaires wore sturdy uniforms generally consisting of a linen undershirt and a woolen tunic. Each was protected by a cuirass of metal strips, a metal and bronze helmet with cheek and neck guards, a leather apron to deflect blows against the groin, and a long, oblong shield curved around his body. Footwear consisted of heavy leather sandals sometimes lined with fur or wool.

Training was intense, often with heavy practice weapons which provided the legionnaire with ample physical strength in actual combat. Marches were long, demanding, and well organized. Supply lines were flawless as was the preparation of overnight camps, miniature logged fortresses erected on the spot. Tactically, Rome took the art of warfare to unprecedented levels. At Alesia in 52 BC Julius Caesar finally surrounded Vercingetorix, the valiant Gallic leader. More than 65,000 Romans had besieged more than 80,000 Gauls using circumvallation, the building of offensive trenches around an entrapped city. Aware that a force of 250,000 Gauls were approaching to relieve their leader, Caesar ordered another set of trenches dug to defend their siege. This brilliant combination of circumvallation and contravallation in the same campaign not only held back the attacking Gallic hordes but forced Vercingetorix to surrender. It was a masterpiece of tactical planning. The Roman Empire at its apogee ran from Scotland to Egypt and from Portugal to Syria.

After the fall of Rome and the rise of the Byzantine Empire, Italy slowly became divided into several powerful city-states which waged war amongst themselves or against invaders from across the Mediterranean. Sicilians, Neapolitans, Genoese, Milanese, and others developed advanced military tactics. Many were considered at one time or another to be the best mercenary soldiers of Europe. From 1416 to 1718, Venice alone fought nine wars against Turkey and five against Milan. When the Risorgimento movement for the liberation and unification of Italy finally triumphed, the armies of Savoy, Piedmont, Sicily, Sardinia, and other parts of Italy were amalgamated into the Italian army but held onto several traditions that still remain.

Clad in well-pressed, dark blue gala uniforms and sporting their distinctive wide-brimmed, plumed hat, the Bersaglieri are probably the most well known Italian soldiers. In June 1836 Capt. Alessandro Evasio Ferrero, the Piedmont Marquis Della Marmora, considered the European battle strategy to be in a stalemate and finally created his ultimate solution. Great, slow troop movements in quasi-static positions, as in Waterloo just two decades earlier, proved too dangerous now that artillery had become more lethal. A well-placed shell could decimate a large number of troops in seconds. With the approval of the high command, La Marmora set out to organize his new light infantry troops, which were to be flexible, agile, and able to fight in small groups equipped with modern weapons. The chosen men were strong and lean with a prowess for gymnastics. Their nimbleness proved useful at Goito Bridge in 1848 during the Italian Revolution. The Italian spearhead had stopped as it reached the partially destroyed bridge. Undaunted, the agile Bersaglieri rapidly crossed over the precarious parapet and successfully engaged the Austrians at their baptism of fire. At Governolo, a small Bersaglieri section simulated a much larger force through a cacophony of trumpets and shouting. The terrified Austrians fled the field unaware that they greatly outnumbered their Bersaglieri foes.

Movement was the Bersaglieri's primary characteristic. La Marmora made sure his troops were never still. Marching was always at a trot and every order had to be carried out on the double. Even at attention the Bersagliere was still in movement as the thick mane of feathers on his hat would dance with the lightest wind. Impressed by the then black-clad Bersaglieri standing before him, Prussian general Moltke told the king, "They carry the color of death but are the most faithful expression of life."

Bersaglio is Italian for target, and La Marmora made certain his Bersaglieri were the top marksmen on the Italian peninsula. European hunters had the custom of plucking a feather from a downed fowl for their bonnets. Soon jaeger units primarily in the Prussian and Austrian armies were doing the same. Some accounts state that the Bersaglieri were such good marksmen that they soon had manes of feathers hanging from their hats. Even their helmets

"To me the guards!". The Grenadiers turn the tide at Goito.

carry the cock feather mane, making their appearance truly unique. The hat is low and light with a brim wide enough to protect a man's neck from the sun and rain. Upon inspecting his troops one day, Colonel La Marmora came across Sgt. Guiseppe Vayra wearing his hat tilted diagonally across his head with his left ear showing and the right side over his eye. As the sergeant hastily began to fix his hat, La Marmora shouted, "Hold still! Let me have a better look. This is excellent! The Bersaglieri will wear it like this. It will give them a mischievous air that I like!"

Another of La Marmora's innovations was a high-precision, rapid-action needle gun which much enhanced the small units' firepower. Peninsular troops joined the French and British expeditionary forces to Crimea and fought particularly well at Sevastopol alongside the guards and the French foreign legion. It was at that bloody battle that the Bersaglieri marksmanship proved its worth and gained great admiration. At one point they allowed the Russians to approach terribly near before devastating their ranks with expertly placed fire. Unfortunately the Crimean War also took the life of Papa La Marmora, as the colonel was known to his beloved men.

In 1870, the Bersaglieri spearheaded the assault on Rome's Porta Pia, entering the capital and finally freeing the eternal city. A statue of a charging Bersaglieri still faces the famous entrance to the city with a simple inscription: "From the people to the Bersaglieri."

The unit fought extensively in all the Italian colonial wars, primarily in North Africa and in the eastern Mediterranean, but also in the Far East where they faced the Chinese Boxer Rebellion along with other troops from European, U.S., and Japanese protectorates. The Bersaglieri flag is the most decorated in the Italian army with thirteen gold, twenty-one silver, and fifty-two bronze medals.

In World War I, Italy fought a bloody war of attrition against the Austrians. It was in that conflict that Enrico Toti, a young Italian, perfectly embodied the spirit of the Bersaglieri. Time and again he returned to the recruiting station intent on becoming a Bersagliere. Time and time he was refused. Enrico Toti had only one leg. Finally, the officers made him a rare concession. Riding a special bicycle alongside the troops he repeatedly fought the enemy until, at an attack near Veneto, he found himself defending an important position. After using up his final rounds against the attacking throngs, he threw his crutches at the Austrians in a last act of defiance.

World War II was an unpopular war for the Italian army which fought with largely obsolete weapons and training. Spirits were at a low. The Bersaglieri fought tenaciously, however, particularly in the North African desert and on the Eastern Front. Germany's top strategist, Field Marshall Erwin Rommel, once said, "the German soldier has amazed the world, and the Bersaglieri have amazed the German soldier." Unfortunately Italy's overall war effort casts a gloomy shadow over those units that fought bravely and well. After liberation, the Twenty-eighth and Thirty-third battalions fought on for the Allies, maintaining the right to keep their traditions.

Italy's northern border is composed of a solid wall of towering, snow-covered peaks. From ancient times, the staunch northern tribes resisted invading armies, tenaciously hanging onto their small mountain enclaves. The Roman Empire could not beat them nor could later European kingdoms. In 1690, a small band of 370 mountain men held back the powerful combined armies of the king of France and of the duke of Savoy through the efficient use of a complex system of trenches and mountain ramparts.

In 1872, Capt. Guiseppe Perruchetti recruited these hardy northerners to create his mountain corps, the Alpini. Formed to defend the northern borders against France and Austria primarily, the Alpini were trained to withstand sub-zero temperatures, to climb seemingly impossible cliffs, and to operate on foot in snowed-out conditions. The Alpini recruits came from the mountain villages of the Alps and Dolomites and had been experts on skis and with climbing tackle since childhood. Climbing for pleasure, chasing mountain goats across dizzying precipices, and dangling from ropes over endless drops had all been part of their adolescent lives. Even before their military service began, the Alpini were already in their element. Dressed in ordinary infantry fatigues, the Alpini were distinguishable only by their heavy mountaineer boots and their distinctive truncated cone felt hat with one eagle feather for an officer and a crow feather for the men. The feather holder was a woolen tuft in the battalion color and the cap badge was a flying eagle with an Alpini horn superimposed over crossed rifles

Although active throughout the end of the nineteenth century, the Alpini troops saw their finest hour in WWI. Defending hundreds of miles of the dangerous snow-covered mountain border with Austria, the Alpini guarded every mountain pass, glacier, and summit against enemy infiltration. The simple expedient of manning one's station was a life-or-death situation. Many men were lost to avalanches or buried inside glacier crags and crevasses. Provisioning was performed against unbelievable odds and thick enemy fire. Yet the front was maintained and the campaign raged for four long years. The Alpini mountaineering skills allowed them to operate in altitudes that would have been impossible for normal infantry troops. As

Bersaglieri troops charge through Porta Pia to take Rome. Painting by Michelle Camarano.

Troops of the Monte Rosa Alpini Division in the opening days of WWII.

great climbers, they often managed artillery pieces, observation equipment, fuel, and supplies over vertical terrain. Combat was constant and brutal with daily artillery barrages and intensive patrols at high altitudes. The Alpini were particularly good at lassoing rocky crags from below to aid their climbs. In many instances the Austrians would cut the ropes. More often than not, however, the Alpini would send up decoy ropes weighted down with rocks and surprise the enemy from behind. Many of the campaign's battles were fought above 10,000 feet (3000 meters), such as those on Monte Nero, at the Adamello, at the Ortler, and at the Laguzoi.

The Alpini of WWI were simple men who had inherited the faiths and superstitions of their ancestors. They believed in mountain legends such as vampires, hobgoblins, witches, and fairies. They also believed that Christ had died for them and that the saints looked over their shoulders. Their battalions are named after the mountains and villages they defended. In WWII, the Alpini fought mainly in Greece and Albania, but many were sent to the Russian front. After the armistice, several Alpini units fought alongside the Allies. Today, the Alpini continue defending Italy's northern mountains and are among the best-equipped mountain units in the world.

Just outside Rome lies Forte Pietralata, an old bastion for the defense of the capital now in use by another of Italy's most traditional regiments, the Granatieri di Sardegna (Sardinian Grenadiers). Although most of the old fortifications have given way to modern buildings and armored vehicle hangars, the center square facing the parade grounds is still the ancient command blockhouse. Inscribed in large lettering over the bunker entrance are the words *"A me le Guardie,"* "To me, the Guards," an ancient reminder of a memorable battle.

Created by King Carlo Emmanuelle (Charles Emmanuel II) in 1659, the Granatieri fought early on when the Piedmont army joined the Austrians in defending the young Austrian queen of Savoy, Marie Therese, from ambitious Franco-Spanish eyes. On 19 July 1747, seven thousand Italian, Austrian, and Swiss troops defeated a twenty thousand-strong Franco-Spanish army at the Colle Della Assietta. So exultant was the Italian commander that, with the battle won, he proceeded to strip the beautiful red and white lapel loops from the beaten Spaniards' uniforms and placed them upon his men's uniforms. At Cosseria Castle, in 1796, the Granatieri held back Napoleon's invading armies until they finally fought to the last man after a desperate siege. In 1848, the Granatieri fought the great Risorgimento battle of Goito against a large, well-trained Austrian army. After a bad start for the Italian forces, King Vittorio Emmanuelle rallied his guards calling, "To me, the Guards, for the honor of the House of Savoy!" As if charged by a bolt of lightning, the Granatieri charged the Austrians, turning imminent defeat into a smashing victory.

In WWI, the Granatieri fought on the northern borders and were instrumental in acquiring Trento and Trieste from the Germans and Austrians. In nearby Veneto, on the mountains at Monte Cengio, there is a cliff known as the Salto dei Granatieri, or the Grenadier's Defilade. Here, in a horrible action during the great war, a squad of Granatieri was trapped and encircled by Austrian mountain jaegers. Instead of taking prisoners, the Austrians slowly pushed the young Italians at bayonet point toward the gaping precipice edge. In a sudden, desperate move, the Granatieri rushed forward, grabbing their attackers in a deadly embrace, and plunged down the abyss to their death.

Today, the Granatieri are part of the honor guard at the Quirinale, Rome's imponent presidential palace. They are also a central unit in the defense of the capital. Deploying in M-113 armored personnel carriers, the Granatieri are known as the Soldati della Capitale, Soldiers of the Capital, and their characteristic Trussed Moor badge is a common sight on Roman streets.

Aside from the army, Italy has an important paramilitary police force known as the Carabinieri. Named after their short, grooved-barreled rifle, which was incredibly effective and accurate, the Carabinieri have maintained law and order in the most remote corners of Italy for more than 150 years. At one time, lone Carabinieri officers faced great dangers from roving country bandits who often fought with brutal methods. Today, although well-organized, trained, and equipped, the Carabinieri still face terrorist groups and the particularly dangerous Sicilian and Calabrian underworld organizations: the Mafia and the Camorra.

Although primarily concerned with internal security, the Carabinieri have been mobilized for every war Italy has fought. At Udine during WWI, German general Von Berrer, the commandant of a German corps, was shot dead by two Carabinieri officers when he entered the town thinking it free of enemy troops. During WWII, the Carabinieri fought on all fronts. After the armistice, a brave Carabiniere, Brigadiere d'Acquisto, constable of the small village of Palo Laziale, took the blame for a raid on German troops to save twenty-three civilian hostages from being shot. At Fiesole, five Carabinieri were shot after offering their lives in exchange for those of their civilian brethren.

Today the Carabinieri perform police duties throughout the country. An elite, handpicked unit of the Carabinieri are the Corazzieri or Cuirraseurs. Selected from men with many years in the unit and impeccable security credentials, the Corazzieri perform escort and guard duty for Italy's president and occasionally for visiting dignitaries. Measuring no less than 6 feet, 3 inches (1.90 meters) and clad in shiny 1876-style cuirasses, dazzling helmets and spit-polish black boots, they are immediate crowd-pleasers as they ride their majestic thoroughbreds through the streets of Rome. The Corazzieri of today would make their founder, King Vittorio Emmanuelle, proud of the corps he created. Along with the Granatieri and the Lancieri di Montebello, Italy's elite cavalry unit, they help guard the presidential buildings. Responsible for NATO's southern flank throughout the cold war, Italy has emerged as a strong ally of the western democracies.

"If the Italian army were made entirely of Bersaglieri, I would conquer the world!" Such was Guiseppe Garibaldi's respect for Italy's crack infantry. (Above) Always on the move, the Bersaglieri march is a brisk trot. (Left) Black cock feathers are also worn on helmets. (Following spread) Impressed by the Bersaglieri fighting in the Crimea, a thankful Turkish general offered a red fez and a curved Turkish sword both of which are still in use today.

MARINELLI
CARANGELE

The Granatieri di Sardegna are Italy's most well known guard unit. (Facing) In tune with the times, their bearskin berretone hats have been replaced by wholly synthetic fur. (Above) Selected from among the army's tallest recruits, the Granatieri use 1848-style gala uniforms. The regiment's famous Trussed Moor badge comes from the four attempts made by Moorish armies to conquer the island of Sardinia. Captured by the islanders, Moorish prisoners were blindfolded before having their heads chopped off, impaled, and paraded on stakes through the streets of Cagliari, the island's capital.

L'aquila
penne

(Facing) Alpini troops on parade below the Gran Sasso range in central Italy. It was from these mountains that Benito Mussolini was whisked to temporary safety by a crack German paratroop commando unit led by Otto Skorszeny in the dying days of WWII. Although similar to graffiti, the writings on the far wall are the battalion's name and area of operations. (Left) An officer checks the line. (Above) An arctic camouflage-clad Alpini aims his Beretta 7.62-mm BM 59 rifle.

The Carabinieri are Italy's paramilitary police force. Unlike the army, they are all regulars and highly specialized troops. (Bottom left) A Carabinieri band performs at the Vatican on a holy day. (Left) Corazzieri and a Carabinieri motorcycle patrolman. Note the pristine, first-class Moto Guzzi bike. (Above) Helmets and cuirasses are kept in mint condition by the units' own goldsmiths. (Facing) The Corazzieri are handpicked for presidential duties. Often older officers and NCOs with perfect records are granted the honor of serving at the Quirinale.

Nearly all Italian military units maintain age-old traditions. (Above) The Elite Mechanized Brigade, the Lancieri di Montebello, formed in 1977, dates its heritage from the Battle of Montebello where Italian cavalry repeatedly charged the Austrians during Italy's second War of Independence. (Facing) The light-blue cavalry cape and black velvet busby are the identifying characteristics of the regiment. (Left) Gala dress of the artillery corps. (bottom) The head of Medusa is a common sight on uniforms originating in the nineteenth century.

SPAIN
La Guardia Real

Spain has been a battlefield for nearly all her history. Overrun by the Roman Legions and taken by the Visigoth hordes, the Iberian Peninsula then saw more than seven hundred years of Muslim domination. The indomitable fighting spirit of the Spaniard, however, never faltered.

Perhaps the greatest exponent of Spanish medieval bravery was the much romanticized wandering warrior, Don Rodrigo Diaz de Bivar or El Cid Campeador (the Cid). His title, stemming from the Arabic *al sayyid* (master chieftain), was granted to him by his Muslim foes. This leader of valiant Christian forces personified the Spanish obsession with a unified Christian Iberia purged of the Muslim infidel. On 17 June 1094, the Cid finally took the Mediterranean stronghold of Valencia after a brutal twenty-month siege. He held the city against numerous Muslim attacks and died undefeated in 1099.

By the twelfth century, the joint Spanish kingdoms finally decided that a total *reconquista* or retaking of Iberia was possible. Yet three hundred more years of bloodshed proved necessary. Slowly, Christian might and organization pushed the Muslims back throughout the peninsula. The Spanish armies were becoming increasingly efficient and battle-hardened. The fourteenth century saw the emergence of the famous corps of *jinetes* or horsemen, elite mounted knights capable of turning the tide in difficult battles. Clad in colorful garb with armor decorated by countless plumes and feathers, the Spanish knight was a sight to see. His training was similar to that of his French and British counterparts but included several light cavalry skills, including mounted bullfighting to train both man and horse.

As the wars progressed, Granada on the towering southern Sierra Nevada became the last bastion of Muslim power. It was a powerful kingdom with tough, well-trained infantry, cavalry, and bowmen. Warfare was to the Muslim mind an intricate science. Granadan tactics were based on the famous Middle Eastern *furusiyya* training manuals which foresaw every possible aspect of war, from logistics and provision to the construction of battlements. Perched on high hills overlooking deep valleys, Granada's network of fortresses was nearly invincible.

The unification of the kingdoms of Castile and Aragon under King Ferdinand and Queen Isabella finally allowed the Spaniards to create a consolidated front against Granada. Thorough planning and extensive training and preparation of troops were undertaken for the massive final blow on the great Muslim fortress. In April 1491, the Christian forces began a long siege with slow, choking movements against parts of the city fortress. Santa Fé was built on the western approaches to the city, blocking the final links Granada still maintained with the outside world. Artillery and firearms, used for the first time in large numbers, pounded the walls, giving much-needed range advantage to the Spaniards. Facing starvation and humiliation, Sultan Mohammed XI, better known as Boabdil, finally surrendered against the will of his people, allowing the Spanish troops into the sumptuous Alhambra palace. On the cold day of 6 January 1492, seven centuries of Muslim presence in Iberia were finally over.

With the Moors beaten, Spain could now concentrate her finances on the rising quest for seaborne discoveries. In fast succession Columbus, Magellan, and countless other explorers blazed the seas, claiming distant lands for the Catholic kings. Led by obsessed conquistadores, Spain rapidly gained enormous amounts of territory.

In Mexico in the early 1500s, Hernando Cortes burned his ships after landing at Veracruz to prevent his men from believing they might return home. He then transformed them into a small, disciplined army and set out to conquer the vast Mexican interior. With light cavalry, small artillery pieces, and an infantry armed with long, two-edged swords, crossbows, and a number of harquebuses, his men were able to take on large groups of natives whose weapons were limited to clubs, axes, slings, bows and arrows, and rudimentary javelins. More than 40,000 Aztec warriors were thus beaten by only 600 Spaniards with just fifteen horses and fourteen guns. In no time Cortes conquered Tenochtitlan (now Mexico City), the capital of the Aztec Empire. The Aztec emperor Montezuma II believed the invaders were descendants of the god Quetzolcoatl and allowed them to enter the city unmolested.

From Panama, Francisco Pizarro led an expedition to Peru and, after climbing the Andes, came upon the Inca city of Cajamarca. After befriending Emperor Atahualpa, Pizarro led him and 3,500 of his men to the city's central square. Once his trap had been set Pizarro exhorted the Inca chieftain to embrace Christianity. Upon refusal, Spanish sharpshooters strategically placed around the square opened fire from all sides while Pizarro seized Atahualpa. Unopposed, the Spaniards advanced on Cuzco, the Inca capital, terrorizing the Incas who greatly feared the horses and guns of the conquistadores. Completely demoralized, the Inca Empire crumbled.

The long wars against the Moors had provided Spain's soldiers with great military experience. The combined use of artillery, sappers, infantry, and engineers in the taking of Granada melded the new fighting concepts developed by the Spanish armies. In the sixteenth century, Spain's tercios led by the great captains such as Gustavo de Cordoba, "el Gran Capitan," ruled the battlefields of Europe. Picking up where the English bowmen and the Swiss pikemen had left off, the tercios made great use of concentrated firepower combined with the mass and shock of the pike. Composed of some 3,000 men, the tercio had a solid square of pikemen with "four sleeves" of musketeers at each corner of the square. After firing a concentrated volley at the enemy ranks, the musketeers would march backward in perfect discipline to reload, while the pikemen advanced to capitalize on the damage done by the musketry. Almost immediately, the second sleeve would be in position to fire, thus compressing the enemy. A series of tercios operated together in wedge or diamond-shaped formations giving each other mutual protection. The famous Flandres Tercios remained unbeaten in Europe for more than one hundred years.

Aside from participating in numerous wars and conflicts in Europe and the colonies and enduring several civil wars at home, Spain's next truly major conflict occurred in the early 1800s when Napoleon's troops became masters of the Iberian Peninsula. On 2 May 1808 the Spanish people rebelled against Napoleon, who had named his brother Joseph Bonaparte king of Spain. The ensuing war was brutal. Defeated at Bailen by Spanish troops under General Castaños, the French were fast to regroup and fight back in a bloody war that would last six years, involving the French against the British and Portuguese allies in the west and the ferocious Spanish irregulars throughout the Peninsula.

It was during the Peninsular War that the term *guerrilla* (little war) entered military terminology. Irregular warfare was used extensively and effectively by the whole of the Spanish populace against the French invader. Organized in *partidos,* civilians attacked the French troops without quarter or mercy.

Much in use by the Spanish guerrilla was the *garrot* (garrote), a long lance with a pointed hook at its extension. Commonly used to down bulls with a violent twist of the neck, it was brutally used against French infantrymen by special bands of *garrochistas*. In fact, the widespread use of terror in the Peninsular War, both by the Spanish irregulars and by the French forces, prompted both sides to recognize the need for restraint.

The Peninsular War also served to ignite a series of uprisings in Spain's South American colonies. One by one, Spain's New World territories wrested themselves free in a series of long and costly wars of independence. Several tough years of internal revolutions ensued before the great Spanish debacle of 1936, including the Carlist Wars, fighting in North Africa, Central America, and the Philippines. Communist victory at the polls led right-wing garrisons to revolt, initiating four years of the most passionate warfare ever witnessed.

From Spain's Moroccan enclave of Melilla, Gen. Francisco Franco, a brilliant military mind who reached the post of general at age thirty, led his mainly Spanish foreign legion troops into the mainland where he was joined by a succession of revolting troops who termed themselves "nationalists." Facing them were the "republicans," a left-wing coalition of anti-Fascist troops which included volunteer brigades from the United States, Britain, and France. The Fascist governments of Mussolini and Hitler supported Franco, while Soviet Russia rallied to the republicans' cause. Soon Spain became a testing ground for the most modern weapons and tactics available to both sides. The Spanish Civil War was brutal, completely devastating the country, but on 28 March 1939 it finally ended with Franco's victory.

Remaining neutral during World War II, Spain was isolated from the world scene until 1975. When King Juan Carlos I ascended to the throne along with a newly elected government, modern Spain came into being. With the new king came a new version of the Royal Guard, El Regimiento de la Guardia Real, Spain's age-old keepers of the kingdom. The Spanish king lives in the magnificent palace of El Pardo in the verdant hills just outside Madrid. The 2,000-strong Guardia Real is lodged around the palace in the huge complex of barracks formed by the Quartel del Rey, the Quartel de la Reina, and the Quartel del Principe. It is composed of volunteers selected from the best recruits the Spanish military has to offer.

Well equipped for its guard duties, the Guardia Real comprises elements from the Spanish army, navy, and air force as well as an expertly trained motorcycle unit riding state-of-the-art Harley Davidsons, a police dog-handling unit employed for guard duty and for bomb detection, and sections representing each of the various corps of the Spanish forces. The Guardia Real is subdivided into three main branches. The first group is composed of the Escuadron de Lanceros del Rey (The King's Own Lancer Squadron) with two sections of light blue clad, mounted lancers in impressive dragoon uniforms dating from Alfonso XIII's cavalry and one section of coraceros or cuirassiers in elegant dark blue and shiny cuirasses. Both lancers and the coraceros form the Escuadron de Escolta Real (Royal Escort Squadron), which first saw action in northern Spain during the third Carlist War. The escort traditionally rode two paces to the right and left of the monarch and half a horse-length behind him. Today, the skills needed for such horsemanship are still visible as the sections march past in dancing step, a truly wonderful sight.

A light horse artillery section completes the mounted portion of the first group. La Seccion de Artilleria Ligera (Light Artillery Section) is composed of two 1906 Schneider .75/.28-caliber pieces in perfect working order, complete with ammunition carts pulled by gargantuan Hispano-Breton horses. Also part of the first group is the small halberdier *zanguanete* or section of the Real Cuerpo de Guardias Alabarderos, perhaps the piece de resistance of the entire guard. Clad in impeccable eighteenth century uniforms and halberds, they are the closest bodyguard corps of the guard. Formed in 1504 as the personal escort of King Ferdinand the Catholic after a thwarted attempt on the sovereign in Barcelona, the Alabarderos keep close watch both inside and outside the royal palace. They were initially known as La Guardia Española, the Spanish Guard, or La Guardia Amarilla, the Yellow Guard. They have kept the king company on all the important dates in Spanish history. They were the turning factor in the *Noche Tragica,* the Tragic Night of 7 October 1841, when rebellious troops of General Espartero's tried to kidnap the infant Queen Isabel II under orders of her uncle. Fighting from the vantage of the main palace staircase, the halberdiers were able to hold back the invaders until the young queen was safely away.

The second group of the Guardia Real is composed of regular troops of Spain's army, navy, and air force. The Grupo de Soldados Reales is composed of three subunits: the Compañia Mar Oceano of the Spanish navy in honor of the old companies of Naples and the famous Tercio del Mar Oceano which brought much glory to Spain in the XVI century; the Compañia Plus Ultra from the air force, named in honor of the first transatlantic flight from Palos de la Frontera to Buenos Aires by three Spanish aviators; and the Compañia Monteros de Espinosa of the army. The Escolta Real protected the king when he left the palace and the Alabarderos guarded the stairways, galleries, and hallways of the palace. The Monteros de Espinosa, created by the sovereign count of Castile in 1013, were a select group that stood guard over the private rooms of the palace. According to legend, Doña Oña, the king's widowed mother, was in love with the Moor Almanazor, who was then enjoying the hospitality of the count, and tried to poison her son while under the spell of her Arab lover. The count's *montero* (squire), Sancho Pelaez, a nobleman from the town of Espinosa in the mountains of Castile, discovered the plot and hastily took the poisoned chalice from the king's hands. In recognition for his deed, he was entrusted with the direct protection of the king and was ordered to choose a guard of twelve honest men from the village of his birth who would be known thereafter as the Leal Real Cuerpo de Monteros de Espinosa (The Loyal Royal Monteros de Espinosa Corps). The army contingent of the Guardia Real honors this special guard of yesterday.

The third group of the Guardia Real is a logistics battalion. Committed to the protection of the royal family, the Guardia Real encompasses essentially all of the country's armed forces, providing a spectacular display of military drill on every festive occasion in the Spanish nation.

GUARDIA REAL

After the young volunteers have received their blue berets for completing their tough basic military training in the field, the entire Guardia Real turns out at the Esplanada Reina Sofia (Queen Sofia Esplanade) for the ceremony in which they will pledge allegiance to the flag, promise to the king, and swear unto God. (Previous spread) The Alabarderos steal the show. The Spanish kingdoms of Castile and Leon are visible in their uniforms as is the fleur-de-lys of the Bourbons. On the halberd blade are the date of manufacture and the initials of the current sovereign. (Below right) The dog-handling squad watches for bombs and trespassers on the royal grounds. (Top right) Men of a regular Compañia de Fusiles clad in 1909 Spanish army uniform and the famous Ros hat. They carry the Mosqueton FR 8 7.62-mm a local replica of the 1956 Mauser rifle, a weapon of incredible accuracy.

Lanceros and Coraceros represent Spain's cavalry in the Guardia Real. When entering the guard, an officer automatically loses three posts, thus a lieutenant colonel becomes a lieutenant. There are but two colonels and one lieutenant general, the king himself.

FRANCE

Legionnaires,Colonials and Metropolitans

The French Foreign Legion
The First Regiment of Spahis
The Garde Républicaine

Few countries fought as many wars as France. Set in the heart of western Europe with strong neighbors all around her, France has been at the center of nearly every major conflict since the ancient Gauls fought the legions of Rome. It was the Franks under Charles Martel, "The Hammer," who stemmed the Moorish tide sweeping northward from Spain in 732. At Poitiers, the ferocious charges of the Muslim warriors lasted more than two days but were met by closed ranks of Frankish soldiers who hacked down both men and horses with axes and broadswords. Charles the Great, or Charlemagne, followed with his mounted knights and built a great empire that spread from the Pyrenees to the Danube. With his death in A.D. 814, the Frankish Empire weakened, and it was only due to the brave rallying of the bishop of Paris that the great city resisted a violent Viking siege in 885-86.

In the north, Norman warriors decisively defeated the Saxons at Hastings, laying the foundation for modern England. Norman power gave way to the Crusades and a long period of Anglo-French warfare. Under King Charles VIII, during his 1494 campaign in Italy, the use of gunpowder finally made its mark on warfare, changing the course of combat. The Spanish Tercios' decisive defeat at Rocroi in the Thirty Years Wars opened the way for French military predominance in Europe. In the age of the "Great Captains," the French military masters — Louis de Bourbon, duke of Enghien; "The Great Condé," hero of Rocroi; and Henri de la Tour d'Auvergne, "The Great Turenne" — paved the way for military engagements that would endure for more than one hundred years.

In the American Revolution, French generals the Marquis de Lafayette and the Comte de Rochambeau led well-trained French troops in support of the American Continental Army, gaining the decisive victory at Yorktown. The bloody French Revolution, which culminated with angry mobs heroically taking the Bastille prison on 14 July 1789, led the way to the rise of Napoleon Bonaparte, who would completely change the spirit of the French army.

French Poilús *man Hotchkiss machine guns from a defensive position. WWI.*

In no other period of her history was France as powerful and feared as during the Napoleonic years. Led by the brilliant Corsican strategist, France's conscript "Grand Armée" became a versatile military machine which gathered experience and battle laurels that would forge practically all subsequent military traditions of the French army. The colors and imperial eagles carried high in battle; the clearly distinguished corps of grenadiers, cuirassiers, chasseurs, dragoons, and Hussars; and the well-organized training and logistical backing created an amazingly strong esprit de corps, making Napoleon's army one of the most consistent and trustworthy ever seen. Before the end of the Napoleonic Wars, his veteran guards had marched into every major European capital except London.

After arriving from Corsica, Napoleon swiftly rose in the French ranks. In just eight weeks, due to his brilliant achievements at the siege of Toulon, he rose from captain to general. Three years later, he led an army and, four after that, was the ruler of France. The Battles of Marengo, Borodino, Austerlitz, Jena, and Wagram remain deeply embedded in the French psyche as perhaps the greatest French feats of arms ever.

Napoleon's military brilliance lay mainly in organizing his various army corps into separate flexible units that could rapidly join into a larger framework. His artillery and cavalry were held in reserve and moved as needed in crucial moments and places of battle. His strategy consisted mainly of forcing a decisive battlefield engagement and using his flexible formation in a concentrated steamroller that in one surge forward marched, struck, and pursued the enemy without pause.

No French victory has ever been as commemorated as Austerlitz, 1805. On the eve of battle, as Napoleon emerged to review his troops, they remembered it was a year to the day of his crowning as emperor in Paris's Notre Dame Cathedral. Gathering brands of hay, the men lit makeshift torches and cheered, "*C'est l'anniversaire, Vive l'Empereur!*" while he strolled triumphantly through their ranks.

Out in the distance, the Austrians and Russians braced for the following day's battle. Victory was swift and decisive. Forcing the Austrians to retreat over the frozen waters of the Satchan Mer after taking the important Pratzen Heights, Napoleon bombarded the thin ice with twenty-five guns, destroying more than two thousand enemy soldiers along with thirty-eight gun teams. To this day 2 December is commemorated solemnly at Saint-Cyr Coëtquidian, the French military academy in Brittany. In fact, the school's parade ground is known as Le Pratzen in honor of those strategic heights, and the school's calendar begins in December, the month of the celebrated battle. Austerlitz also remains in the streets of Paris, not only as the name of the city's central railway station, but on the majestic Place Vendôme column, built with the melted iron of the captured cannons.

Napoleon's impetus, however, was stopped at Waterloo, where the age old saying, "*La Garde meurt et ne se rend pas*" (The Guard dies but never surrenders), was finally disproven. The French army survived, however, and with the Second Empire of Napoleon

III, great victories over the Austrians in Italy, at Magenta and Solferino, maintained the status of France's fighting men. Several campaigns overseas in the Crimea, Africa, Mexico, and the Tonkin forged a colonial army that would bear the brunt of France's fighting until the German onslaught of 1870-71 reached Paris, sparking the bloody Paris commune fighting of 1871.

France structured its army in three distinctive categories: the Armée Metropolitaine, composed of mainland troops; the Armée d'Afrique, composed mainly of foreigners, Pieds Noirs, as the Frenchmen born in North Africa were called, and the Penal Battalions of unwanted criminals; and the Armée Coloniale formed of indigenous troops from the colonies such as the goumiers from Morocco, the Tirailleurs Senegalais from Senegal, and Algerians among others. It was the struggles of these troops that formed the historical regimental traditions enduring today.

The First World War was perhaps most bloody on French soil. Germany's offensive caught the mighty French army off guard and the slaughter of the first few weeks of war dispelled any hopes that the conflict would be swift and decisive. Instead, a long bloody stalemate would ensue in which a few yards of fiercely contested terrain would be grasped at an immense cost of human lives only to be lost to a similar assault in a matter of hours.

The first major confrontation at the Marne from 5 to 10 September 1914 saw more than 2,000,000 German troops attempting to breach the Allied lines in northeastern France. The more than 1,300,000 French troops under Marshal Joseph Joffre held them back, fighting with their backs to their beloved capital. On 7 September, Paris was in range of Germany's monster howitzer, "Big Bertha." At any moment a breakthrough could wedge past the French lines and clinch the conflict. Yet in a famous incident, the mayor of Paris commandeered the city's fleet of more than six hundred taxicabs and ordered them to ferry reinforcements to the front line. The French army held the line and by 10 September, the German onslaught had been contained. The Marne reversed Germany's offensive in Belgium and France and forced her to adopt a defensive posture in order to regroup for the next stage of the war.

In February 1916, the chief of the German general staff, Gen. Erich von Falkenhayn, unleashed an offensive at Verdun in order to "bleed France white" and force her out of the war. More than two thousand artillery pieces on both sides turned the French countryside into a lunar landscape of craters and mud. French fortifications such as the Fort de Douaumont and the Fort Vaux under constant fire could only be reinforced by a narrow, forty-mile (sixty-five-kilometer) dirt road aptly called "La Voie Sacrée" (The Sacred Way). Yet French general Henri Phillipe Petain's promise that "*Ils ne passeront pas*" (They shall not pass), was upheld by the French troops, and the German posture soon became defensive. At that moment, the French troops attacked, putting into practice a new technique. The "creeping barrage," developed by artillery specialist Gen. Robert Nivelle, advanced infantry behind a forward-moving wall of artillery fire. Verdun was a bleeder for France. It lost 542,000 soldiers from February through December 1916. It bled the German army as well, however, and of their 434,000 casualties, 120,000 were lost in a single week.

Verdun gravely affected France's military spirit, and it may have led to the disaster of the early years of World War II, when the failure of the Maginot Line and General Petain's change of heart led to the great nation's darkest hour under Nazi domination.

Yet not all was lost for France with Hitler's invasion and the creation of the vassal state of Vichy in the country's southern half. Gen. Charles de Gaulle's Free French and the Maquis, or French Resistance, never let go, and rescued the honor of the country's fighting men. As the Allies began to reverse the tide of the war, the French army again collected much deserved honors, at Bir Hakeim in the Western Desert, at Cassino in Italy, and at the liberation of Paris and Strasbourg. General LeClerc, after bringing his light column from Chad and attacking the Italian-held Oasis of Koufra in Libya, vowed he would not stop until he placed the French flag on the steeples of Notre Dame and the Cathedral of Strasbourg. His Second Armored Division ensured the general's promise and to this day a French flag flies from each church's tower.

In the south of France elements of the three armed forces fought together for the first time, landing in the Riviera and Provence, advancing to the north and northwest. A new French army was slowly being developed. It would, however, have to pay its dues before becoming the professional fighting force it is today.

After WWII, France had to fight a bloody guerrilla war in Indochina. Although mobile forces rushed to explosive zones such as the Red River Delta were successful under Gen. Jean de Lattre de Tassigny, in the end the traumatic defeat at Dien Bien Phu marked the end of French involvement in Indochina. More than 60,000 Viet Minh troops led by General Vo Nguyen Giap held the siege for fifty-five days, slowly encroaching upon the 15,000 crack French troops in the air-land compound near the Laotian border. One by one the outlying defensive positions fell to concentrated artillery and human wave assaults that would leave almost half the attackers dead. For the first time, a local guerrilla force defeated an elite colonial army in a set battle. This led to an upsurge of guerrilla movements worldwide.

In Algeria, the local Front de Libération Nationale began a nationwide terror campaign designed to secure independence. The French army reacted swiftly and decisively, putting into practice the lessons learned in Indochina. For the first time, helicopters were used in battle, as French strategists familiar with the Algerian Djebel (Algerian Desert) after 130 years of domination employed large Sikorskys to outflank the guerrillas in the rugged Algerian cliffs and valleys. In the cities, tough French Paras rapidly unveiled the mysteries of Algiers' Casbah and smothered a murderous urban terrorism campaign. Although in the field the French were pushing the FLN into hiding, politically leverage was granted toward an independent Algeria. It was an enraged and frustrated French army that finally left Algiers in 1962.

With most of its vast empire now independent, France still maintained several small overseas garrisons of foreign legion and Infanterie de Marine troops. In recent cases the French army has had to act swiftly, and it did so with growing professionalism. In 1978, responding to a sudden attack by Zairian guerrillas on copper mining sites in eastern Zaire manned mainly by Europeans, the Second Foreign Legion Parachute Regiment executed Operation Leopard, a daring jump into the village of Kolwezi. After driving off the murderous Katangese guerrillas, they rescued more than two thousand European survivors.

More recently, French armored troops participated in the liberation of Kuwait, guarding the allied's left flank in the thrust into Iraq. Active in the United Nations peace-keeping efforts, French troops are practically everywhere the blue-helmeted troops are engaged, including Cambodia and the Balkans. Although modern and rapidly maturing into one of the most proficient forces in the world, the French army has not forgotten its traditions.

The French Foreign Legion

There is no regiment in the French army that evokes such awe and mystery as the French foreign legion. Considered by many to be a haven for desperadoes, political refugees, broken-hearted lovers, adventurers, and petty criminals, the Legion Etrangere is in fact one of the most traditional elite fighting forces in history. As an institution, the legion has long been wary of outsiders. Its rigid five-year contract and the *anonymat*, or offer of a new identity, still attract young hopefuls from every walk of life who are eager for a new start. More than 150 nationalities compose the legion, and of the circa 8,500 men 80 percent are foreigners.

It was King Louis Phillipe who created the legion on 9 March 1831. Its objective was to rid France of unemployed or dangerous foreigners who could become a nuisance to the nation. The legion would be sent to Algeria and by law would not be employed in France proper. The Old Legion, as it was later known, was formed mainly of Germans, Swiss, Belgians, Italians, Spaniards, and Poles driven from their countries by political persecution or economic strife. In Algeria, the men were formed into battalions composed of each respective national group, and soon trouble with the local Arabs kept them busy.

A revolt by Abd el Kader, the young emir of Mascara, led more than three thousand armed horsemen to the gates of Oran in 1832. Several charges were broken down until finally the French counterattacked, routing the attackers from the city. Particularly impressive was the Fourth Battalion, composed of Spaniards, most of whom had fought as guerrillas in the Peninsular War against Napoleon. Ruthless and unorganized, they were, however, skilled and courageous warriors. In battle, they would slip beneath the attacker's horse's belly, surprising and grasping the rider, pulling him to the ground, where he would be stabbed to death by a waiting companion. Several legion victories in Algeria ensued, but no success sufficiently impressed the French mainland to change the spartan lives the men led in the desert.

In Spain, the dying King Ferdinand VII willed his throne to Isabella, his three-year-old daughter, represented by her mother

Paris taxis assemble to ferry troops to the front at the Marne. 1914.

Maria Cristina. The king's brother, Don Carlos, sought the throne for himself and, raising an army, began the bloody Carlist Wars of 1835-38. Unable to contain the rebels, the Spanish kingdom sought assistance from France, Portugal, and England. France contributed by transferring the foreign legion to Spanish command. The more than five thousand men who landed in Spain in 1835 fought the bloody conflict virtually unsupported by the government in Paris, which insisted that responsibility for pay, clothing, and food lay with the Spanish kingdom. The war was brutal and many legionnaires eventually changed sides. On one occasion, an outpost defended by some thirty legionnaires was captured by the Carlists. When asked to change sides, however, the legionnaires refused. For this they were dragged behind the enemy's horses from one village to the next, naked, with their hands bound behind their backs, and their eyes plucked out. After unbelievable suffering, their ordeal was finally ended with a pistol shot. Needless to say, when the legion found their bodies, they wanted revenge. Captain Ferrary soon captured a group of Carlists and extracted the legion's payment in kind.

On more than one occasion, legionnaire fought legionnaire, but at the olive groves of Barbasto on 2 June 1837 the struggle was particularly bloody. A German officer watching from the Spanish side later wrote, "The soldiers recognized each other, they called each other by their names, and then shot each other heartlessly." It was in Spain that legion units were reorganized and nationalities were mixed to increase flexibility, end rivalries between battalions and allow for easier command with French as a central language. This would leave a lasting spirit in the legion. In rags, hungry, and diseased, five hundred survivors of the original five-thousand-man detachment finally crossed the Pyrenees into France at the end of the war. The legion had been reduced to a beaten handful.

Amazingly, however, the legion did not die. A new legion was quickly formed in southern France, and two battalions were sent to Algeria in early 1837. Just off the ship, the legion was sent to participate in the assault on Constantine, a well-defended Arab fortress perched on a towering plateau surrounded by impassable ravines. After four days of brutal fighting, the legion breached the walls and engaged the defenders in bloody house-to-house fighting. By the end of 13 October, the last enemy flag was captured.

Fighting in Algeria continued throughout the first half of the 1800s, and although most of the country was pacified after the defeat of Abd el Kader's 45,000-man army at the Isly River, remote areas such as the mountainous Kabylia region remained ablaze with rebellion.

In 1856 a large French offensive was mounted to finally defeat the Kabyles who had resisted all foes since Roman times. Even Abd el Kader had been unsuccessful there. For eight months the French marched forward, defeating all opposition until they reached the ridge of Ischeriden. On 24 June 1857, the Second Régiment Étranger (2nd RE) advanced against the 4,000-5,000 entrenched Kabyle defenders. With General MacMahon on the lead the legionnaires advanced as if on parade, with rifles shouldered. The baffled Kabyles held their fire, not knowing what to make of the strange French move. Suddenly, bayonets were flung forward and the legion charged. The Kabyles responded with heavy fire, but it was too late. Algeria was conquered and secured.

In France, the king had been replaced by the short-lived Second Republique which ended when President Louis Bonaparte, nephew of the great Corsican, proclaimed himself Emperor Napoleon III in 1851.

Two years later, France joined a British and Sardinian expeditionary force to the Russo-Turkish border in the Crimea, answering a call for help by the Turks, who had been attacked by Tsar Nicholas I. Nicholas was intent on obtaining control over the Bosphorus, thus obtaining free access from the Black Sea into the Mediterranean. On 14 September 1854 the allies landed in the Crimea and scored an immediate victory over the Russians at Alma. They then besieged the powerful fortress of Sevastopol from where the Russians were preparing to attack Constantinople. What initially seemed like a swift walkover turned into a nightmare with the arrival of winter. Freezing cold and the outbreak of cholera ravaged the allied lines and extended the siege for a year. Thousands were lost to disease and Russian bullets.

In May 1855 the 1st RE made a frontal assault on the fortress but was beaten back. Another allied assault in June left more than six thousand casualties in the fields of fire. On the night of 7-8 September the bearded legion *pioniers*, or sappers, built ramps and scaffolding with scaling ladders and wooden planks. When the French troops arrived at dawn, the path was in place and they achieved a swift breakthrough, pushing the defenders back from the Malakov and Redan strongpoints overlooking the fortress city. By nightfall the Russians began evacuating Sevastopol. A year later, the war was over.

Napoleon III then dispatched the legion with the bulk of France's army in Italy, where in support of the Carbonari (Italian unionists), they defeated the Austrians at Magenta and Solferino.

Three years later, the legion was sent across the Atlantic to Mexico, where they were tasked with protecting the government of Napoleon III's puppet emperor, Maximillian III. Landing at Vera Cruz in March 1863, two battalions of the foreign legion were eager to join the siege of the Juarist capital of Puebla in the interior. Instead they were assigned to patrol the malarial, swampy, coastal plains where cholera and yellow fever would eventually take a huge toll on the troops. A railroad line was being built from the coast and several work camps lay along its path. Guerrilla leader Antonio Diaz had been the terror of the region, attacking these small camps and massacring their garrisons. On 20 April he came upon a camp defended by the legion. Not only were the raiders turned back, but Diaz found his death at the hands of Prussian lieutenant Milson. It was the subsequent action, however, that would become the supreme example of legion bravery: the defense of Camerone.

French Paras deploy from a Sikorsky in the Algerian Hills.

One month after arriving in Mexico, Colonel Jeanningros, the legion's commanding officer was informed of the arrival of an important convoy carrying food, ammunition, and more than three million francs in gold for the siege of Puebla. To protect the convoy on its route from the coast, the Third Company was detached. Since all officers were sick with fever, Captain Danjou, a wooden-armed veteran of the Crimean War, volunteered to command the column and was followed by young sous-lieutenants Vilain and Maudet. Only sixty-two men were healthy enough for the march. Losing no time, the small force left late at night. After resting at the legion garrison of Paso del Macho, the troop passed the ruins of the abandoned farm hamlet of Camarón, later immortalized in French as "Camerone."

Unknown to Danjou, word of the convoy had leaked to the Juarists, and a 2,000-strong cavalry force led by Col. Francisco de Paula Milan had been deployed to ambush it. This troop had located the small legion force and stalked it from the time it left Paso del Macho. By morning, advance patrols of both forces finally met. The legionnaires were just beginning to brew coffee when the alarm was given by the sentries. Danjou immediately saw that he would be unable to resist on open ground and ordered his men to fall back on the walls of Camerone. Watching from the distance, Milan realized that such a hasty retreat could only mean his troops had been spotted. If he was to catch the French on open ground he had to be swift. Like thunder, the Mexicans charged, but the French formed into a square and fired at a mere sixty yards (fifty-five meters). The fusillade broke the attack, allowing the legionnaires to reach the small ruins.

A second charge followed immediately but this also was met with a defensive square followed by a brief counterattack. During a brief pause in the battle, the French prepared makeshift barricades and defenses. Six hundred Juarist cavalrymen prepared the third charge of the day. A negotiator was sent from the Mexican side to demand surrender. Danjou's answer was succinct. "Pas de question." No time was lost by the Mexicans, and one of the first hit in the charge was Danjou himself. Mortally wounded, he still had time to hear his men promise that they would fight to the end. By 11 A.M., all food, ammunition, and the last bottle of wine were gone. A second negotiator was turned back by the legionnaires. The legion fought on throughout the day. By 5 P.M., only twelve men were left standing. Colonel Milan's voice could be heard during a lull crying shame that his two thousand could not defeat a fistful of Frenchmen. A final all-out attack followed.

After fierce hand-to-hand fighting, Sous-lieutenant Maudet, Corporal Maine, and legionnaires Catteau, Constantin, and Wenzel were the only ones left, fighting with their backs to a corner wall. When their last rounds had been fired, the five lowered their bayonets . . . and attacked! Maudet was hit by rifle fire and Catteau, who had thrown himself in front of his officer was hit nineteen times. The three survivors stood before the final volley. In the nick of time, however, Mexican colonel Combas held back his men and offered a final surrender. Maine replied that the only acceptable terms would be to surrender with their weapons and the tending of their wounded. "I can refuse nothing from men like you," replied the colonel. When Colonel Milan rode up to examine the scene, he asked, "Is this all that is left?" and when informed, he said, "Then these are not men but devils!"

While the battle for Camerone was raging, the French convoy passed by unmolested and aided in the taking of Puebla, which soon fell to the French. The emperor, accepting a request by Colonel Jeanningros, decreed that from then on the name Camerone would be inscribed in the regimental standard. It remains on all standards and colors of the legion. Every year, at every legion detachment around the globe, 30 April is commemorated as a sacred day for the legion. At Aubagne, the legion's main barracks in southern France, Captain Danjou's wooden left hand is paraded before the troops as an icon from that distant battle. At Camerone a monument was built with a fitting inscription: "Here stood less than sixty men facing an entire army. Its weight overwhelmed them. Life, rather than honor, abandoned these soldiers of France."

In September 1883 the legion was send to Tonkin, the northern province of the empire of Annam, modern-day Vietnam. Upon disembarking from their troopship after a long voyage, they were greeted by the energetic General de Négrier and his now famous address: "You legionnaires are soldiers in order to die, and I am sending you where you can die." The country, considered a French protectorate, had been ravaged by organized groups of pirates known as Pavillons Noirs (the Black Flags). Supported by regular Chinese troops from across the northern border, they proved to be a cunning foe.

Admiral Courbet, the French expedition commander, immediately organized operations to take the enemy strongholds of Son Tay and Bac Ninh. At Son Tay, more than 5,000 French troops charged the stockaded fortress held by 20,000 Chinese and Black Flag irregulars. Several attempts were turned back until Corporal Minnaert, a large Belgian *Fionier*, burst forward swinging an axe and, after jumping over the moat, pushed himself into a breach in the wall to grab an enemy flag and scream, "Long live Belgium, Long live the Legion!" The Chinese were so stunned by the effect Minnaert's action had in rallying his men, that they fell back. A fierce bayonet charge won the day. After the battle, while rewarding the brave Belgian with the military medal, Admiral Courbet confided to him that had he waved the French flag, shouting "Vive la France!" he would have been given the Legion of Honor.

Almost two years later, some six hundred legionnaires found themselves under siege in an old Chinese fort at Tuyen Quang. Outside the ramparts, 20,000 Chinese troops prepared the assault. Slowly and patiently, the Chinese mined and sapped the ramparts. A complex network of approach trenches reached the walls, and artillery barrages kept the French defenders away from the approaching earthworks. Finally the Chinese breached the outer wall. Inside however, they faced the bearded sappers of the foreign legion, who had built an enclosed wooden palisade to fall back to sixty yards (fifty-five meters) behind the ramparts. With grappling hooks, the Chinese finally brought part of the palisade down, but as their engineers made way for their infantry, they were met by a lightning French bayonet counterattack that drove the intruders out of the fortress.

Two days later, the Chinese attacked again under cover of a moonless night. By dawn their efforts had again been defeated by the staunch legionnaires. Four days after that, more than 200 pounds (900 kilograms) of explosives sent the last piece of wall flying into the air as the Chinese prepared a final attack. Desperate hand-to-hand fighting erupted, but the timely arrival of a French relief column finally drove the Chinese hordes away. Ragged but proud, the defenders formed up inside the fortress and presented arms to their relief column, an act that would become a tradition in Indochina for the next seventy years.

In the north, next to the Chinese border, Chinese regulars consistently penetrated the French lines held by marine frontier posts, conducting hit-and-run raids. When Colonel Galliéni, the French area commander, complained about the incidents to his Chinese counterpart, Marshal Sou, he was offered the reply, "Unfortunately, I have lost control of my men. But if you catch them, shoot them. Don't worry about a trial." Of course no Chinese troops were ever caught, so Gallieni replaced the marines with legionnaires, who soon began conducting their own raids across the Chinese border. When Marshal Sou complained to the French area command, he was politely told by Galliéni that, "Unfortunately, these men are foreigners and are totally out of my control. But if you catch them, shoot them. Don't worry about a trial." Not only did trouble across the northern border end, but Marshal Sou commended the French colonel by saying that he could have been born a Chinese.

The next conflict that involved the legion took place in Dahomey on the African coast. Initially friendly to the French, local king Behanzin had been convinced by German agents to create an army to combat French interests in the region. His African troops were numerous and included full battalions of local women warriors dubbed by the French "Les Amazones." These in fact were the most fierce of Behanzin's troops. They fought valiantly in countless hit-and-run attacks against the French column, which was advancing through the thick jungle toward the inland capital of Abomey. Native troops even flung themselves from overhanging trees at the unsuspecting French bivouacked next to the Dogba River.

As the legionnaires slowly pushed the local troops back, a messenger from King Behanzin finally appeared before the brilliant French expedition commander, Colonel Alfred Dodds. The messenger stated that his king had sent a warning that "the shark that will eat the French" would soon arrive with more than 12,000 troops and artillery. Undisturbed, Dodds replied to the messenger, after showing him a pile of African bodies killed in the last attack. "If you are the shark who eats the French, then I am the whale who eats the shark." It was a terrified messenger who rushed back to Abomey. When the French entered the capital a few days later, they found it virtually empty. Among the souvenirs taken back to Algeria from the royal palace was a white parasol decorated with fifty human jawbones.

In Madagascar a bit later, a French expedition marching through the jungle failed to learn the lessons from Dahomey and were ravaged by disease and exhaustion, prompting a French medical officer to state, "When a French soldier goes into hospital it is to be sent home. An African tirailleur goes in to be healed. A legionnaire goes in to die." Of the almost six thousand French dead, only twenty died due to injuries sustained in combat.

After so many valiant instances when the legion defended the Tricouleur, it was still seen by the French command as a conglomeration of lowly troops. Their action in North Africa never ceased, and slowly that region became the legion's beloved home.

In Morocco during the opening days of the twentieth century, mounted companies were formed to pursue rebel warriors. Although horses could not be requisitioned by the legionnaires — their officers feared they might encourage more desertions than the accepted numbers — the two-man mule proved to be a secret weapon. Each mule carried the full load of two men and six days worth of rations, consisting of *kessra* (a hard Arab wheat biscuit), dried dates, fodder, and several water bottles from which the mules had been taught to drink by the legionnaires. The men took turns riding and in this manner they could cover up to forty miles (sixty-five kilometers) a day. Suddenly the legion could move across the desert with unprecedented speed.

In Europe, trouble was brewing and, with the assassination of Archduke Francis Ferdinand at Sarajevo, the Great War of 1914-1918 began. More than 44,000 legionnaires fought with distinction during World War I, including many Germans, Bulgarians, Austro-Hungarians, and Turks. The Régiment de Marche de La Légion Étrangère (RMLE), the legion's marching regiment, fought with such bravery that in only three years it became the second-most-decorated unit in the French army, earning the double fourragère of the Legion of Honor and the Croix de Guerre 1914-1918 worn today by their descendants at the 3ème Régiment Etranger d'Infanterie (REI) in French Guiana. Most legionnaires from the Central Powers were left behind to defend the French North African outposts, which they loyally returned to their brothers in arms after the cessation of hostilities, but many saw combat in Europe. In fact, the most decorated NCO in the French army during the First World War was Sergent-Chef Mader, a German legionnaire.

The inter-war years were relatively quiet although the legion saw plenty of action, particularly in Morocco against Abd el Krim. Under Marshal Hubert Lyautey, France's brilliant resident-general of Morocco, military action gave way to the building up of the country and intelligent cooperation with the local population. At Foum-Zabel, pioniers of the 3ème REI were ordered to build a tunnel through a small mountain of solid granite. With picks, shovels, and crowbars, the bearded pioniers went at it with vigor. Once the 200-foot-long, 25-foot-wide, and 10-foot-high (60-meter-long, 8-meter-wide, 3-meter-high) tunnel was completed, a simple inscription was carved into the rock: "The mountain barred our way. We received the order to pass nonetheless. The legion carried it out."

WWII caught France unprepared and the German onslaught rapidly reached the gates of Paris. Legion troops fought bravely to stop them, particularly around Verdun, but eventually were forced to fall back with the bulk of the French army. After Dunkirk, most of the men of the 13th Foreign Legion Half Brigade (13ème DBLE) who had fought valiantly in the Narvik expedition in Norway escaped to join the Free French forces in London. They were soon sent to Africa where, after a brief strike against Vichy forces in Dakar, they sailed round the continent and struck at the Italians in Eritrea, where they defeated a 14,000-man garrison at Massawa.

Not all legionnaires joined the Free French, however, and on 20 June 1941 in Syria, the 13ème DBLE's forward scouts came across legion elements of the 6ème REI, who held Kadam, a suburb of Damascus. A brief fusillade ensued with casualties on both sides. As the 13ème arrived before the Vichy legion's positions, the bugler was ordered to play "Le Boudin," the legion's marching song, to regroup. From the defensive stronghold, the 6ème's bugler returned the song in a bizarre prelude to a battle that saw legionnaire poised against legionnaire, as at the olive groves of Spain more than a century before. Luckily, the 6ème was replaced with line infantry, avoiding the tragic encounter. With Syria freed, the 13ème joined the Free French Brigade, manning the defensive Gazala line across the Libyan-Egyptian border, blocking Rommel's crack Afrika Korps from Alexandria and a certain victory in the Western Desert.

The southernmost tip of the Gazala defenses alloted to the Free French was given the nickname, the "desert of the desert." Daylight temperatures reached more than 120° Fahrenheit (49°C) in the shade, and water was nowhere to be found. Nights were freezing and sandstorms enveiled men and equipment with a thin crust of sand. It was precisely in this desolate flank that Rommel concentrated the bulk of his attack. Intending to strike through the southernmost protections while a feinting head-on attack kept the British busy, Rommel was confident that he could drive past Bir Hakeim and catch the Allies from behind.

After four months of tense waiting, straining to see movement in the desert stillness, the defenders at Bir Hakeim heard the rumble of enemy tanks. An initial Italian attack was beaten back, while more than thirty tanks burned before the camp. More Axis troops were captured when supply columns entered Bir Hakeim, mistaking it for an Italian camp. Rommel decided to swing wide, avoiding Bir Hakeim, to thrust into the British rear. General Koenig, the French commander, ordered raiding patrols to harass the German convoys as they passed around his position. All seemed well until the Italians finally breached the British line north of Bir Hakeim, transforming the compound into an island amidst the advancing Axis armor.

For fourteen days, the French resisted non-stop bombardment by artillery and aircraft. Water began to run low and was rationed to three pints (1.7 liters) a day. Having stopped a great part of the enemy forces long enough to allow the British to fall back to their second defense at Alamein, General Koenig ordered a nighttime attack rather than surrender. On the night of 10 June the French broke out fighting to rejoin the British line. Almost 2,700 of the original 3,600 men made it to safety. Bir Hakeim would live forever as one of France's most brilliant feats of arms.

In the Far East, having fought a Japanese-backed Thai attempt to take Cambodia, the French were forced to accept Japanese occupation in their Indochinese territories. Although liberated by Allied troops, the French army continued the struggle against the rebel Viet Minh. The mainstay of France's defense in Indochina was provided by legionnaires, a great number of whom were ex-Wehrmacht Germans. Almost half of the 22,000 troops killed in Indochina were legionnaires. Indochina was the most costly war for the legion, surpassing both World Wars in casualties.

At Dien Bien Phu, the final debacle, psychological warfare was constantly attempted by the Viet Minh with good results among the indigenous troops defending the base. On Camerone Day 1954 perfect French sounded from powerful loudspeakers placed at the jungle fringe. "Why continue to resist?" the Viet psy-ops officer said. "Why repeat what the legionnaires did at Camerone — get massacred to the last?" The ploy was beginning to have an effect on some North African and Thai defenders, but when legion Lieutenant Colonel Lemeunier began reading the Camerone story over the camp's public address system, one by one, more than 1,000 men throughout the positions began singing "Le Boudin," completely overwhelming the Viet propaganda attempts.

A total of 6,328 legionnaires were taken prisoner at Dien Bien Phu and sent on the famous death march to Viet internment camps. Only 2,500 returned.

The fall of Algeria left a lasting impression on the foreign legion. Sidi-Bel-Abbès, some fifty miles (eighty kilometers) south of Oran, had become the legion's sacred home. Legion traditions throughout the years had deep North African roots. When the commandant of a legion unit arrives at a ceremony, for example, the band

(Facing Page) The Musique Principale of the foreign legion attached to the 1er REI performs beneath the Eiffel Tower guarded by a watchful pionier. Drummers carry their drums lower than most military bands. Note drum covering with the Latin legion motto, *legio patria nostra* ("The legion is our home"). (Left) Only the top six graduates of Saint-Cyr are given the opportunity to serve with the legion. When officers on attachment from other French units return to their regiment, they are allowed to wear one legion button on their tunics to identify them as men who served with the legion. The legion's sole general and a high-ranking colonel take a break. (Bottom Right) When the Musique plays the "Marche des Éclopés" ("March of the Wounded Ones"), an old march from Napoleonic times played so that the wounded could participate in parades, the drummers tilt their bodies on every roll. (Bottom left) Legionnaire of the 3ème REI. Note the fourragères drooping off the right shoulder.

(This Page Top) Legionnaires are posted in French bases around the globe. In French Guyana on the north-eastern tip of South America the Legion trains for Jungle Warfare, and protects Europe's Ariane Space Project. (Bottom) Armed with Italian repetition shotguns, or FAMAS rifles, the Legion provides France with a powerful deterrent. (Facing) A young Caporal clutches his FAMAS at a jungle outpost. This light 5.56 mm automatic rifle is 30 mm shorter than the M 16. It is made of plastic and composite materials and can fire in single mode or in bursts of three or continuous shots. It can also fire 500 gram anti-tank or anti-personnel grenades. The weapon can easily be converted for firing with either left or right shoulder as the cheek piece can be rapidly removed and turned around exposing an ejection opening on the opposite side. The bolt is then removed and the ejector is switched to the other side.The whole operation takes a few minutes.

(Facing) The Garde Républicaine is the last mounted unit in the French army. It consists mainly of one cavalry and two infantry regiments. Its main missions include escort and guard duties with France's president (This Page) and foreign dignitaries. While the infantry wears the classic shako headgear, the cavalry dons a shiny cuirassier-style helmet. The horse's mane not only adorns the helmet but also serves to protect the neck and upper back, deflecting saber strikes downwards.

RAÏMA
DU SPAHIS

68140013

-(Previous Spread) The spahis employ the AMX RC 10 armored vehicle, armed with an 105-mm cannon and possessing a fantastic hydraulic suspension system which allows the vehicle to raise or lower itself according to the terrain, or to fall upon any one of its four extremities to increase its firing angle. It is amphibious and extremely comfortable, earning great praise during Operation Daguet, the French thrust into Iraq.

—North African traditions such as the *tenue orientale* or Arab uniform (Top) or the regiment mess sign (Bottom) are alive and well with the spahis.

(Left) In cavalry light blue and red kepi, this young soldier represents France's lasting colonial forays. (Above) Proudly displayed at spahi barracks in Valence is this desert-camouflaged Iraqi T-55 brought back from Desert Storm. (Facing) For centuries the Tricouleur was raised under North African skies. It is only fitting that traditions are maintained by the French army.

- The French army has developed into one of the most modern and well organized military forces on earth. (Above) Officer cadets from the military academy of Saint-Cyr Quotétiquidian in Brittany, proud in their *cassoar* headgear, parade down the Champs Elysées. (Left) A member of the École Polytechnique, France's prestigious Military Technical Institute founded 1794. Among its famous members were soldiers such as field marshals Joffre and Foch, scientists A. Fresnel and H. Poincarré, industrialists such as the famous carmaker André Citröen, and even President Giscard d'Estaing. Among the important projects developed at the Polytechnique are the TGV, France's high-speed train; the Airbus Jet Consortium; France's Civil Atomic Energy program; and Ariane, the European Space project. (Facing) French cavalry carries the *fanion*, a badge bordered by horse's hair on the tip of a spear. This tradition originated in North Africa, where it was common to cut off the tail of a defeated enemy chieftain's charger. It can be made either with black or white hair; white, however, only if the regiment's commander has been killed in battle.

BRAZIL
The Independence Dragoons
The Corps of Naval Fusiliers
The Presidential Guards Battalion

Since Portuguese explorer Pedro Alvares Cabral discovered Brazil in 1500, Brazil has grown to become the largest country in Latin America. Portuguese domination was not achieved without bloodshed. Although the Portuguese were friendly with most local indians, foreign privateers and military expeditions soon ravaged the vulnerable 5,000-mile (8,000-kilometer) coast. French, Dutch, Spanish, and English galleons and men o'war sailed Brazilian waters, occasionally raiding the small Portuguese outposts, forming alliances with local tribes and encroaching on the land.

The local indians inhabited the whole coastline and, although primitive, had mastered the use of stone, wood, and fire. Most were nomadic hunter-gatherers and great warriors. Their weapons were the mace, heavy clubs, such as the <u>tacape</u> (a typically Brazilian club, larger and spiked on four sides,and decorated with feathers) and the large <u>uirapara</u> bow made of a hard flexible wood. To shoot it, the indians sat on the ground and, with one foot supporting the center of the bow, were able to shoot large arrows with incredible precision.

For hunting and raiding, the indians also used a smaller bow with arrows tipped with sharp bone or teeth. Feathers were placed symetrically at the back of the arrow, enabling it to fly in a rotating movement similar to a modern rifled projectile. Tips were dipped in the juice of poisonous plants and therefore had to be carried in a pouch. Extremely skilled with the bow and arrow, the indians could easily kill at up to 328 yards (300 meters). Iron Wood javelins called <u>murucús</u> were also used, as were blowpipes called <u>zarabatanas</u>, which shot small darts with incredible precision. Shields made of tapir or manatee skin offered some protection, but the fighting skill of each warrior was what counted above all in their savage wars.

Fast movers through dense jungle, strong-bodied and capable of long marches carrying heavy loads, Brazil's indians had a highly developed sense of smell and hearing. Wars were waged not for territory, but generally to avenge a tribe member killed and eaten by an enemy or for the capture of women. Most actions involved ambushes in clearings or on jungle trails, but villages were also attacked.

Well defended ones had palisades and, with the wind in the right direction, attackers often lit fires into which they threw great quantities of red pepper. The result was a primitive type of tear gas that often forced the defendants to run for air.

When two strong groups faced each other, each made terrifying screams before battle, in order to demoralize the enemy. Many indians would also throw their arms into the air to appear larger, flex their muscles and show each other human bones and necklaces made of human teeth.

Arrows began flying and the two forces would charge, closing in for a savage battle. With blows of the <u>tacapes</u> and javelin thrusts, bloody encounters would rage until one group would abruptly retire. Prisoners were killed and eaten in a festive war ceremony.

No part of the human body was wasted, except for the brain, which the indians would not touch. Cannibalism was more often due to vengeance than gluttony, although early Portuguese settlers were told that the meat had good taste.

After befriending most of the tribes, the Portuguese soon had to defend their newly conquered land when a strong French fleet arrived in 1557 at Guanabara Bay,intent on building what they called <u>La France Antarctique</u>, at what is today Rio de Janeiro.

A bloody eighteen-year conflict began. The French befriended the fierce Tamoio tribe and fought tenaciously against the Portuguese and their Tupi indian allies. Through the mid and late 1500s numerous conflicts between the Portuguese and French broke out at several points along the coast.

British and Dutch pirates also made raids, hiding their ships and booty in the numerous coves. Yet Portuguese determination never faltered.

When the legendary British pirate Thomas Cavendish attacked the settlement of Espirito Santo, he found an abandoned village. Advancing to the inland convent of Penha where the townsfolk had fled to prepare their defense, the pirates were hit by a strong volley of harquebus fire.

Neighboring indians rallied by Portuguese missionaries came to the rescue as the English prepared a furious night attack. In order to trick the pirates, the indians and settlers lit fires in the hills around the convent to give the impression that massive indian reinforcements were arriving. This held the attack back until daylight when the convent was better prepared to resist.

When the pirates attacked the villagers were well entrenched and fought back savagely. At exactly that moment, according to local legend, a bright light lit up the sky, and the image of a saint led an armed knight forward to fight off the invaders. The British pirates were pushed back to their ships, leaving the dead and wounded behind.

In 1580 Phillip II of Spain ascended the Portuguese throne, uniting both nations and bringing Portuguese territories the ire of the enemies of Spain. Among these were the Dutch, strengthened by the ten year success of the Dutch East India Company which had bitten into the Iberian monopoly in Asian trade. A Dutch West India Company was formed, with Brazil one of its objectives. In 1624 a fleet of twenty six ships commanded by Dutch Admiral Pieter Heyn appeared off the coast of Bahia and seized the

Dragoons fight fiercely at Rosario Pass.

The Independence Dragoons.

port. A fifty two ship Spanish fleet sailed in reply with 12,000 men to drive the invaders out.

In 1630,the West India Company sent another expedition tocapture the state of Pernambuco in northeastern Brazil, where sugar cane was the prize. After a well planned two pronged attack by infantry and armed launches, the Dutch forces finally took the cities of Olinda and Recife, paving the way for a Dutch enclave in northeastern Brazil. Successive battles ensued on land and sea, and in 1631 Portuguese forces were poised to recapture Olinda from retreating Dutch forces.

Before abandoning the town, the Dutch tried to extract a heavy ransom from the Portuguese as a bribe not to raze Pernambuco's capital. The besieging commander Matias de Albuquerque sent them the answer, "With our weapons in our hands we do not buy, we conquer. What we can give you are musket balls, not boxes of sugar. Burn Olinda if you cannot keep it, we will know how to build an even better one."

Although burned to the ground, Olinda was again in Portuguese hands. But an unforseeable event changed the path of the war. A Portuguese traitor deserted to the Dutch giving them invaluable intelligence. A string of Dutch victories followed. At the small fort of Rio Formoso, twenty men and two cannon opposed a strong Dutch force led by the brilliant General Sigismund Von Schkoppe. The post commander Pedro de Albuquerque, ordered to surrender, replied he would fight to the last man.

Three ferocious assaults were unable to overcome the small but determined force. On the fourth attack the Dutch finally punched through the walls. Inside, not one man was left standing. Upon finding Pedro de Albuquerque lying to the side, wounded, a Dutch soldier moved to relieve him of his sword. "Halt!" cried Von Schkoppe, moved by the resolute defense, "One does not take the glorious sword of a hero."

Pedro de Albuquerque was then cared for and treated with the highest respect by his Dutch captors. He was soon granted freedom in return for a promise to leave at once for Lisbon. He did only to return later.

Dutch territory grew along with their morale, and even successful surprise attacks such as a "commando" operation on Recife by five hundred men under Captain Martim Soares Moreno, were not enough to stem the Dutch tide. Local forces were forced to take to the interior and continue the struggle using their own brand of guerrilla warfare, called Guerra Brasilis (Brazilian warfare).

In 1635 Dutch reinforcements sent to Pernambuco outnumbered those from Portugal and Spain by thirty to one. Pernambuco would have to defend itself with its own troops. Unable to defeat the Dutch in open battle, the locals organized ambush companies whose mission was to destroy cane fields, kill solitary Dutchmen and collaborators, and above all help maintain the flame of resistance.

In 1637 Maurice of Nassau, one of the greatest soldiers in history, landed at Recife as "governor, captain, and admiral of the conquered lands and of those yet to be conquered in Brazil." A legendary strategist on the battlefields of Europe, Nassau was sent by the Company to consolidate Dutch gains and expand the conquestof territory. After only a week in Recife, he organized his first campaign. It finally destroyed the last bits of resistance only three days later.

An intelligent administration with rapid social, economic, and political gains soon brought peace and prosperity to Pernambuco. Tolerance of the local populace and respect for the Catholic religion soon quelled the remaining resistance. The Dutch could now concentrate on conquering more territory.

The following years saw incessant fighting between the Dutch, strongly settled in Pernambuco, and the Portuguese strongholds in Bahia to the south. Although one side was able to occasionally damage the other's economy, no strategic advances were made by either one.

In 1641 news of the restoration of King John IV arrived in Brazil. Now at war with Spain, the Portuguese expected a rapid turnaround in their relations with the Dutch.

Nassau, however, immediately let it be known that although peace was possible, it was absolutely unimaginable to hand back Dutch Brazilian territory. Unable to wage war on two fronts, Portugal signed a ten year armistice with the Netherlands. But the Dutch broke the treaty and rapidly expanded their territories. They finally accepted the treaty.

In the meantime, Brazilian agents were able to move freely through Dutch territory in Pernambuco, laying the seeds of rebellion which was sure to happen once the situation in Europe stabilized.

In 1644 Maurice of Nassau returned to Europe and the insurrection gathered speed. Without Nassau's control, Dutch soldiers and their indian allies soon began a campaign of indiscriminate killing of any Brazilian that fell into their hands.

The Portuguese king offered his support, but saw there was little he could do and ordered insurgent leaders to wait until Lisbon could help. The Brazilians could no longer wait. Disobeying the king, they went into action. Troops began secret training deep in the interior of the country. Others were landed by ship at selected points under pretext of chasing insurgents wishing to break the Portuguese-Dutch peace treaty.

Funds were collected, secret arms and munitions caches set up throughout Pernambuco, and city folk and farmers silently disappeared without notice.

Although plans for a rapid taking of Dutch positions in an insurrection planned for 1645 were betrayed by deserters, the patriot army finally met the Dutch at the Monte das Tabocas battle. In the opening stages, well organized Dutch troops rapidly pushed the young army back almost to their reserve troops made up of unarmed civilians and slaves.

In a desperate gesture, Governor João Fernandes Vieira rallied the men around him and promised freedom to any slave who showed valor in combat. As if on fire, the slaves stormed down the hill armed with rudimentary bows and arrows, lances and machetes. Behind them came the people. The masses fell upon the Dutch lines from all sides forcing them to flee the battlefield leaving one hundred dead and vast quantities of weapons and ammunition.

Slowly the patriots pushed the Dutch invaders back to their strongholds at Recife and nearby forts. Recife was soon besieged, and a long stalemate developed.

On 18 April, 1648 strong Dutch reinforcements arrived and General Von Schkoppe led his men south toward Bahia. His 6,300 men were met by 2,200 patriots in a small group of hills known as the Guararapes. The Dutch expected to find only a token force, and when only two hundred Brazilian soldiers showed themselves, the Dutch charged.

The rest of the defending force remained in hiding as the lightly armed cowboys retreated, leading the Dutch through hillocks and marshes.

When the tight terrain had effectively divided the Dutch troops rendering ineffective their mass of pikes and firearms, the Brazilians attacked shouting “To the swords!” Blacks, indians, and whites charged from all sides in perfect discipline, engaging the Dutch who tried to bring their reserves to the front. After four hours and 1,038 casualties the Dutch retreated. Guararapes was a victory due to the Brazilian's tactic of forcing the enemy to accept a decisive battle in unfavourable circumstances, an advanced idea at the time. By hiding their forces and using surprise and small units, they chose the terrain and terms of battle. The first battle of Guararapes, was not the last. On 17 February 1649 a force of 3,650 Dutch soldiers under Colonel Brinck decided to advance on Guararapes to lure the 2,640 Brazilians there into a decisive battle of their own. They hoped this would allow them to lift the siege of Recife and regain the upper hand. After a forced march, the Dutch troops arrived at the Gurarapes Hills and took up ideal defensive positions in well chosen terrain.

Spotting the enemy's positions, patriots silently infiltrated Dutch lines from passes to the west of the hills on the dark night of the eighteenth. By morning, the Brazilian force was behind the enemy unnoticed. On the afternoon of the nineteenth, under strain because of thirst and fatigue, the Dutch decided to return to Recife since their enemy seemed weak and unwilling to take the bait. As they left their defensive positions, the Dutch were suddenly attacked by the Brazilians from their hiding place behind the lines. Caught completely by surprise, the Dutch army collapsed.

According to Von Schkoppe's review of the battle, “The great majority of our troops ran desperately, letting themselves be killed without resistance, as if they were children.” Only forty eight patriots lost their lives at Guararapes against 927 enemy soldiers. The Dutch mistake was costly and gave the Brazilians their greatest military victory of the campaign. During a subsequent exchange of bodies and prisoners an interesting dialogue occured between the patriot officer, Antonio Dias Cardoso, and his Dutch counterpart, clearly defining the spirit of the war. When theDutch officer said that in the next battle results would be different as they too would fight in spread out formations, the young Brazilian replied, “Then better for us, as in our ranks every man is a captain, while in yours each man needs a captain beside him to win”, referring to the large number of mercenaries in the service of Holland.

In 1654, Recife finally fell to Portuguese Brazilian troops. The Dutch occupation was over. The Dutch however were not the last invaders to try their luck on Brazilian territory. Wars were constant as were conflicts against hostile indian tribes resisting against the growing push westward by adventurers chasing new riches for the Portuguese crown.

Slowly, Brazil's borders began to expand. As the country grew in people and territory, so did the dream of independence. In 1808, driven from Portugal by Napoleon's invasion of the Iberian Penninsula, the Portuguese Regent Prince João VI arrived with his court in Rio de Janeiro from where he would continue to rule. One of his first actions was the Anglo-Brazilian taking of French Guiana on the northern coast of the continent. With no threat of French influence nearby, the king was able to concentrate on developing the infant nation, while supressing a growing independence movement.

After Napoleon was finally beaten, the king returned to his homeland. He left behind his son and heir to the throne, Dom Pedro. With stiff Portuguese reaction to the wish for independence, the situation in the colony became tense.

In January 1822 the Regent Prince Pedro decided to stay in the land he had known for most of his life. To counter the beginning of a revolt by Portuguese troops, the prince called upon his Brazilian officers for support. More than six thousand men, including several priests volunteered to form the prince's army. Portuguese troops resisted the prince and tried unsuccessfully to have him kidnapped and sent to Portugal. On a trip to the southern province of São Paulo, the prince's troops were intercepted by a messenger on the banks of the Ipiranga River with news from Lisbon. Portugal, aware of the tide in Brazil, had vetoed several of his decisions and ordered him back. In a swift act of defiance, the young prince called his escort and tore the ribbon with the green and red of Portugal from his uniform. He shouted the fateful words “Independence or Death!”

Immediately, the troopers of the Imperial Guard of Honor, repeated the gesture, and rid their uniforms as well of the colors of Portugal. The Prince Regent soon became Dom Pedro I, emperor of Brazil. After a swift combination of land and sea attacks on remaining loyalist posts, the young country could finally savor independence.

Brazil consolidated its position as one of the leading powers of South America by fighting several times to protect its sovereignty against its neighbors. In 1864, however, reacting to Paraguay's ambitious leader Francisco Solano Lopez whose troops invaded thepoorly defended southwestern province of Mato Grosso, Brazilian troops prepared for the largest and bloodiest war of its history. Argentina and Uruguay soon found themselves targets of Paraguayan hostility. After large tracts of Argentine territory including the city of Corrientes were taken what came to be known as the Triple Alliance was formed.

Although Argentina and Uruguay contributed both men and means, it was the Brazilian army that would bear most of the fighting. The opening move of the war on 27 December, 1864 was the Paraguayan advance on river and land forces in the sparsely inhabited province of Mato Grosso in southwestern Brazil. More than 3,200 men landed from a powerful river flotilla to the south of the Brazilian advance fort of Coimbra, dominating the heights above the Paraguay River.

Defended by only 140 men, the small garrison held on. Government depots in the nearby city of Corumbá were stacked to the ceiling with rifle cartridges, but the defenders had not received ample supplies. After several attacks on the first day of the war, the men inside the fort could count with only 2,500 cartridges from their initial 12,000. On that tense night, while sentries peered over the ramparts at the enemy filled darkness outside, almost seventy women of the fort led by the courageous wife of Lieutenant Colonel Portocarrerro, the acting CO, set to work while their loved ones got what little sleep they could. Using hammers, steel pipe, and rocks, they adapted the ball shot available to the caliber of the fort's rifles. In the morning, 6,000 more cartridges were on hand for the defense of Fort Coimbra!

The morning attack was violent. Enemy soldiers breached the walls only to have their hands and heads hacked off by the desperate defenders. After the enemy retired to regroup, Colonel Portocarrerro sent a patrol after them. The patrol killed over one hundred of the enemy and returned with their weapons and eighteen Paraguayan soldiers whose wounds were treated inside the fort. With only 1,000 cartridges left, the officers knew the defense was impossible and they planned a silent breakout.

At nine in the evening, the Brazilians quietly slipped away unscathed leaving the Paraguayan wounded behind. When the enemy finally invaded the fort the following day, they found nothing more.

The successful Paraguayan invasions of Mato Grosso, the southern province of Rio Grande do Sul, and the Argentine city of Corrientes were short lived. A decisive river victory by the Brazilian navy at the Battle of Riachuelo on 11 June 1865 turned the tide of the war, and now Paraguay was forced to fight on its own soil.

Once the invaders had been defeated and pushed back from Argentina and southern Brazil,the allies decided to advance up the Paraguay river with naval and land forces to force the Paraguayans back toward Assuncion. Landing at Paso de la Patria, Brazilian General Manuel Luís Osório was the first to set foot on enemy soil, and soon the allies began to prepare to attack the powerfulfortifications of Humaita.

However, the Paraguayan army attacked the unsuspecting allies on 24 May,1866 at their camp by the Tuiuti Lake. More than 56.000 men fought the largest and bloodiest battle South America has ever seen. After only four and a half hours, the Battle of Tuiuti was over. Thirteen thousand Paraguayans and 4,000 allied troops lay dead. This great victory was not fully exploited since the allies did not pursue the retreating enemy. At Tuiuti, General Osório's legendary courage and resolve reached mythical proportions as lance in hand, he led his faithful troops as one of them.

The allies next took the river fortress of Curuzu after a daring landing by Brazilian troops.They hastily attacked the fortified positions of Curupaití to the north, only to suffer a terrible defeat in which they lost almost 4,000 men. Paraguay's well-entrenched troops suffered no more than one hundred casualties.

In early 1867, a new front was opened in the northern theatre with a poorly planned attack from Mato Grosso. A cholera epidemic broke out and Brazilian supply lines collapsed. They retreated through the malarial swamps of Mato Grosso and more than half the expedition perished on the way. The remainder of the army managed to return after thirty five days by hellish forced march with all four artillery pieces and all flags flying. This operation, immortalized as the Retreat from Laguna, allowed the remaining Brazilian troops to regroup.

On the southern front the war raged on after the strategic position at Humaita was besieged for almost two years. Finally at 3 AM on 19 February 1868 the Brazilian fleet tried to force passage through three huge chains blocking the Paraguay River in full view of the fortress artillery in spite of torpedos fired from the banks, and iron spikes buried in the river floor. After monumental artillery exchanges the fleet finally broke through to Assuncion bombarding the city four days later. The siege was maintained and despite several bloody assaults, still held. Paraguayan troops lashed canoes to large water plants called camalotes and tried night approaches to the Brazilian fleet. Some ships were successfully boarded and defended by savage hand to hand fighting but the fleet was able to defeat all attempts. In late July the Paraguayan defenders of Humaita silently fled northward. The great chains were finally cut in three pieces and taken as trophies by the governments of the three nations.

The allies continued their push northward by building a palm tree log road and a small railroad to outflank the enemy batteries at the river fort of Angostura. Instead, the troops entered the swamps of the infamous Paraguayan Chaco, defeated the enemy at the Battles of Itororó and Avaí and completely routed the Paraguayan army from the lower Paraguay river.

Most of the fighting had fallen to the Brazilian army and navy, led by the duke of Caxias, Luiz Alves de Lima e Silva. At the bloody battle for the bridge at Itororó on the Paraguayan rear, theduke of Caxias commanded a now famous attack. The bridge changed hands several times during the day. It seemed like an impossible objective for the Brazilian troops. After a savage Paraguayan counterattack the sixty five year old Caxias, supreme commander of the allied forces,sensed the moment. He unsheathed his sword and galloped to the front of the troops crying, "May all those who are Brazilian follow me!" Cheering wildly, the troops swept over the bridge forcing the enemy to retreat and carrying the day. The sight of the general risking his life a few meters from enemy rifles, sparked an immediate response from the troops as though hit by a sudden bolt of lightning. According to General Dionísio Cerqueira, "Even dying men lifted themselves in a last effort, swords or carbines in hand, only to follow their general for a few steps, before falling dead."

Soon Angostura and Ypacarai were taken and Assuncion, the capital, captured. Although Lopez fled to continue the fight with a token army in the north, he was finally killed fighting Brazilian troops in Concepcion Province in early 1870. The Paraguayan War, or War of the Triple Alliance, was the bloodiest conflict in Latin American history. Paraguay lost four-fifths of its entire male population from disease and the enemy in the largely swampy battlefields. The war elevated the Brazilian army to prominence as a professional and well led institution.

The Paraguayan War, together with the winds of change blowing in from Europe, brought a new spirit to Brazil. On 15 November, 1889, Marshal Deodoro da Fonseca declared Brazil a republic, putting an end to the already decrepit empire. For several years following, the Brazilian army maintained national order, controled revolts throughout the country, and pioneered vast interiors and isolated border areas.

Among the pioneering soldiers, one stands out - Marshal Cândido da Silva Rondon. Responsible for laying telegraph lines through large tracts of Brazilian jungle, Rondon eventually led expeditions to the central and Amazon regions of Brazil. He catalogued a large number of the animals, plants, and minerals, mapped the terrain, staked out borders, and pacified and defended numerous newly discovered indian tribes. His philosophy with regard to the primitive Amazonian tribes, was to "die if necessary, to kill, never!" Leading an expedition 1n 1907 through the jungle, his leather rifle strap stopped a poisoned <u>nhambiquara</u> arrow which would have hit him squarely in the chest. He fired his shotgun skyward, frightening his attackers who would eventually become his friends. On another occasion he needed manpower to cut through the thick forest to install telegraph lines. Rondon was aided by entire tribes he had befriended on previous expeditions. He personified the traditional respect and zeal of the Brazilian army for the country's indigenous tribes. Rondon, now has his name inscribed in the annals of the New York Geographical Society with Amundsen, Perry, Charcot, and Byrd some of the greatest explorers in history.

World War I did not bypass Brazil. After several freighters weretorpedoed off the coast by German submarines, Brazil declared war on the Central Powers. A medical team was dispatched to France, a naval fleet patrolled the South Atlantic and Western African coasts with the Royal Navy and Brazil sent naval aviators to fly under British command.

In 1942 after submarine attacks on its shipping off the Brazilian coast, the country declared war on the Axis and entered World War II. Almost immediately, the northeastern coast became an important haven for Allied shipping patrolling the South Atlantic, preparing the buildup for Operation Torch, the invasion of North Africa.

Several airbases were expanded or built along the strategic coast from which the shortest distance between the Americas and Africa could be flown. Almost overnight, French influence in the Brazilian army was replaced by the United States. Although Brazil dove headlong into its mission patrolling the South Atlantic, scoring hits on marauding U-boats alongside American patrols, it felt its efforts were not enough.

On July 2,1944 the first 5,000 of the 25,000 man Brazilian Expeditionary Force set sail for Naples, where they would join the American Fifth Army in the push for northern Italy. The troops went through a short training period and took their place on General Mark Clark's far left flank. The army slowly probed the heavily fortified Gothic Line in the Appennine Mountains of Tuscany. The green Brazilian troops, relying on obsolete French tactics, received a setback on contact with the battle-hardened enemy.

On a rainy muddy morning in October, slowly advancing Brazilian troops failed to take the German communications center

Brazilian troops storm the fortress at Paissandu.

at Castelnuovo di Garfagnana. Rather than frightened, the poised young soldiers reevaluated their tactics and gritted their teeth for what was to come. They advanced, taking several German positions. The Brazilian line reached the base of a mountain range in which crack German troops were deeply entrenched. General Clark felt he had to take the heights of Monte Castelo dominating the front before the first snows of the winter of 1944 began to fall if the allies were to grab Bologna. An initial American attack, supported by Brazilian artillery, failed miserably, squashed by coordinated German fire. A second American attack met with the same result, bolstering the defenders' morale. A small hillock called Monte Belvedere which offered a good jumping off point forfurther attacks, was taken and secured by the G.I.s. A third attack was rapidly planned for the Brazilians but a swift German counterattack retook Belvedere on the eve, exposing the Brazilians' left flank to German artillery fire from above. Heavy rain and a low ceiling made Allied aircraft unable to support the assault, while deep mud blocked tank support.

At 0700 the troops moved uphill; it would be an all out infantry charge. Although the troops slogged uphill pushing the German picket back, a counterattack by midday succeeded in blocking them. Monte Castelo loomed high overhead affecting Allied morale. But the tougher the German resistance, the stiffer grew the resolveof the Brazilians in the valley below. Monte Castelo was beginning to become a matter of pride.

After the third unsuccessful attempt, the arrival of one of the coldest winters in northern Italian history, cloaked Castelo and the surrounding mountains in a generous coat of snow. The young soldiers from the tropics who had never even seen snow suddenly had to fight a nerve racking duel of probing patrols against the expert mountain troops who held the heights. Although equipped with summer uniforms, a few U.S. winter spares and virtually no knowledge of combat in snowy terrain, the Brazilian <u>pracinhas,</u> or "little privates", fared surprisingly well in the freezing cat and mouse shootouts.

Under constant artillery fire from above they used ingenious measures against the cold. They stuffed dry straw in their combat boots to avoid trench foot producing an incredibly small number of cases compared to the proportions of most Allied units. Burning diesel oil created an artificial fog. The young Brazilian soldiers slowly became battle hardened, holding theirown against the enemy.

With the depths of winter out of the way, a fourth attempt was planned for 21 February 1945. This time the whole Brazilian division, supported by elements of the Tenth U S. Mountain Division would try the ascent. At exactly 0600 hours, the main body of troops from the First "Sampaio" Infantry Regiment began to move up the muddy hill, dodging bullets, mortar fire, and deadly machine gun barrages. Suddenly zooming P-47 Thunderbolt fighters of the First Brazilian Fighter Squadron arrived to the cheers of the advancing troops. From the rear the Brazilian artillery rained shells exploding ahead of the troops.

After twelve long and bloody hours Lieutenant Colonel Franklin of the Sampaio called over the radio set, "I'm at the top!" The Brazilians had finally stormed the crest of Monte Castelo. From there on it was downhill all the way with victories at La Serra and at Castelnuovo against a stubborn but outfought enemy.

In April the Brazilians took part in the Allied spring offensive against the Gengis Khan line on the Po River and Lake Garda, as well as in the strikes against the Alpine passes. Spearheading the

Allied forces, the Brazilians scored a brilliant victory at Montese and held on for two days while U.S. troops caught up, taking Tole and Vergato.

By late April General Mascarenhas de Morais' troops had won honors at Collechio and Fornovo, and on the thirtieth the entire German 148th Infantry Division, remnants of the 90th Panzer Division and what was left over of the Italia Bersaglieri Division, surrendered to the proud young army. They took more than 14,000 prisoners including two generals, 80 field guns, more than 1,500 vehicles, and 4,000 horses. Advancing enthusiastically to the

D. João VI arrives in Rio de Janeiro, 1808.

northwest the Brazilian division was the first Allied army to join advance elements of the French army at the Italo-Franco border.

On May 2 the division halted on word of the German generalsurrender on the Italian front. According to postwar books about the Italian campaign written by Generals Mark Clark, commander of the 5th Army, and Willys D. Crittenberger, CO of the 4th Corps to which the Brazilian division was posted, the Brazilian sector of the Appenine front proved to be the toughest and best defended. Joining American and Canadian troops as the only "American" armies to fight and win in Europe, the Brazilian army contributed to the Allied cause in what was perhaps the most important conflict of all time. At Pistoia,the green, yellow, and blue flag of Brazil waves over the cemetery. Monuments mark the mountain towns through which the Pracinhas slogged during those bleak winter months. This young and inexperienced South American army, through courage and sacrifice, carved a small name for itself in the annals of European warfare.

The Brazilian army returned home to reassume its duties securing the country's sovereignty and pioneering its vast interiors. Led by a well prepared officer corps, it has adapted its size and structure to the realities of the country. Brazil prides itself on a long standing tradition of solving problems through diplomacy, a custom reflected in the fact that it is one of the world's countries which spends the least of its GNP on defense. The advancement of Brazilian society seems to have been the main goal of the Brazilian Army, one of the most powerful forces in Latin America.

The Independence Dragoons and The Grenadiers

On the deep Central Plateau lies the capital city of Brasília, built in 1960 to attract settlers to Brazil's interior. Today a sprawling architectural wonder linked by modern highways to all corners of the nation, it is also the new home of the traditional guard units of the Brazilian army. Perhaps the most visible and famous is the dazzling First Cavalry Guards Regiment, the Dragões da Independência, or Independence Dragoons.

One of the first cavalry units created in the colony for the personal protection of the Viceroys, it traces its origins to the Esquadrão de Cavalaria da Guarda dos Vice Reis (Squadron of the Viceroy's Cavalry Guard) formed in 1763 when the capital of the colony was transferred from Bahia to Rio de Janeiro. It was later organized under the somewhat pretentious title of Squadron of Light Cavalry of the Guard to the Illustrious, His Excellency The Viceroy of State. About the same time, in the interior gold producing province of Minas Gerais, a regular cavalry unit was created to substitute several small dragoon units which operated in the region.

When the Portuguese Regent Prince John VI arrived in 1808 at Rio de Janeiro with his court fleeing Napoleon in Iberia, this Brazilian cavalry became a powerful force. Convinced of the need for a strong mobile cavalry to pursue and destroy an enemy force attempting to land in Brazil, the king created the 1st Army Cavalry Regiment. This was a force powerful enough to deal with any French attack on the new center of the Portuguese empire.

When the king returned to his homeland after the final Anglo-Portuguese defeat of the French, his son the Regent Prince Dom Pedro, and a handful of his trusted Dragoons swiftly broke the chains tying Brazil to Portugal. Young Emperor Pedro I conscious of the conspiracies plotted by the remaining Portuguese loyalists, created the Imperial Guard of Honor, a handpicked cavalry corps which included some of the most capable soldiers in the country, many from the 1st Cavalry Regiment.

The guard took precedence over all other army corps, and its members, under an Imperial decree, "will not salute other than to my imperial person, the empress, my much beloved and respected wife, as well as my august imperial family." Their elegant white uniforms were designed by the French painter Debret, who sought inspiration in the uniforms of the Austrian Dragoons in honor of Empress Maria Leopoldina's Hapsburg origin. The Dragoons, anglicized from Dragon, were named for the short French Dragon musket which these troops carried. They participated in several skirmishes against the remainder of Portugal's Brazilian army, but were soon disbanded in 1832 after the merging of the 1st Rio de Janeiro Cavalry Regiment with the Minas Gerais Regular Cavalry Regiment into the powerful 1st Army Cavalry Corps.

The Argentine-Brazilian War of 1825-28 for posession of the southern province of Cisplatina -modern day Uruguay- featured the 1st Cavalry Regiment participating in the ill fated battle of Rosario Pass, also known as Ituzaingó by the Argentines. Due to this unit's fighting retreat - "never turning its back on the enemy," galloping from column to column defending the rear of the infantry and artillery from the enemy cavalry the Brazilian army escaped annihilation and were able to regroup to fight again.

One day in 1889 Marshal Deodoro da Fonseca had a brisk but fateful exchange with the rebellious troops assembled at Rio's Santana Park. He asked for a horse to ride into the War Ministry and proclaim the new republic. He was immediately given Ensign Eduardo José Barbosa Junior's mount, a bay with the regimental number six, for the ride to put an end to an empire. That horse of the 1st Cavalry, was never ridden again living out its days with the regiment. After an impressive burial it was immortalized in a simple tradition. To this day the commander of the prestigious 1st Cavalry Guard Regiment rides a bay with the regimental number six in memory of the 15th November, 1889.

The 1st Cavalry participated in every great event of the new republic. In 1916 influenced by the "Belle Epoque," it was suggested that an Honor Guard wearing the uniform of the Imperial Guard of Honor be formed by the oldest cavalry unit in the army to protect and escort the president and foreign dignitaries. It was to guard state palaces and make the final charge at 7th of September Independence Day parades.

Although a popular idea, it was unable to break through army bureaucracy until 1927. The charismatic commander of the 1st Cavalry,Lieutenant Colonel Euclydes de Oliveira Figueiredo, was able to get permission from the War Minister. On the 7th of September of that year, the 1st Cavalry proudly left its barracks in Rio de Janeiro's São Cristovão district wearing the red trimmed white uniform and golden scaled dragoon helmet, horsehair falling down the back. The traditional tiger skin shabraque was set as part of the saddle, as was the sabretache in typical dragoon style. The only differences from the original uniform worn on the Ipiranga were a black star on the helmet front replacing the original PI for Pedro I, and the exchanging of the empire's coat of arms on all badges with those of the republic. The new unit was named the Independence Dragoons,and would inspire generations of Brazilians as a symbol of independence.

In 1967, the unit was transferred to the new capital of Brasília. They left for the last time their beloved São Cristovão barracks, but with a feeling of destiny. Commanding the regiment on that day by Colonel João Baptista de Oliveira Figueiredo. The father had led the first departure from barracks, and his son was given the honor of leading the last. The people of São Cristovão lined the streets as the Dragoons left for their new home on the Central Plateau. Young Figueiredo, a brilliant army officer, would eventually surpass his father and honor his regiment by becoming Brazil's president. To this day he maintains a strong link with his old regiment. His retreat in the beautiful mountains of Petropolis outside Rio de Janeiro is appropriately named O Sitio do Dragão, "The Dragon's Lair".

The Dragoons adapted perfectly to their new home. Their eighteenth century uniforms created a delightful contrast to the city's futuristic architecture. Besides hoisting the enormous national flag, the Dragoons form the guard of honor at the ramp of the palace when the president arrives for work Monday morning and when he departs on Friday afternoon. This duty rotates every six months with the Dragoon's infantry brothers from the Presidential Guards Battalion, providing a colorful backdrop to the city.

On the 7th of September the Dragoons perform the final charge, horses galloping, swords whistling in the air, Brazil's historic flags fluttering in the breeze, to a drum and bugle fanfare. It is a short, wonderful moment that reminds Brazilians of the day when the sun of liberty finally shone on Brazil.

Besides the Independence Dragoons of the 1st Guard Cavalry Regiment, ceremonial duties are carried out in Brasília by the traditional Batalhão da Guarda Presidencial, the Presidential Guards Battalion, also known as the Grenadiers. Rotating every six

Marines fought from the ships at Riachuelo.

months with the Dragoons at the presidential palace, the BGP as it is popularly known, evokes images of the Paraguayan War with their royal blue or beige uniform, leather crossbelt and high shako headress. Characteristic of the battalion is the crossbelt used by all officers and a golden pen secured by a chain to a collar guard adorned with the arms of the Brazilian Infantry. A full feather penache and yellow epaulettes distinguish officers from the men asdoes the use of a purple cummerbund under the belt.

Originating with the Batalhão do Imperador, the Emperor's Battalion created by Pedro I in 1823, this unit has participated in almost all conflicts in which Brazil has ever fought. Its first ensign and flag bearer of the new nation, later second in command of the battalion, was Luís Alves de Lima e Silva, the duke of Caxias. The Duke was one of Brazil's greatest military heroes leading allied troops in the Paraguayan War.

The Fuzileiros Navais

Another famous unit is the Navy's Corpo de Fuzileiros Navais, or Naval Fusilier Corps, Brazil's marines. In garance red tunics and blue or white trousers and sporting the famous ribbon cap, they are an elite unit on parade and in combat. The Marines are the striking force of the fleet. They are made up of three infantry battalions, named Riachuelo, Humaita, and Paissandu after the corps' most glorious battles, and of several smaller company sized groups stationed along the Brazilian coast. Together they carry enough punch to be a small army. An all volunteer service, the marines can land on any beachhead and hold their own against almost any enemy. They are able to deploy their own artillery, armored vehicles, transport and support corps, engineering corps, amphibious recon, special operations groups, combat divers, and marine paratroopers. Operating from Brazilian naval vessels, they are one of the most respected forces in all of Latin America.

The Fuzileiros Navais are standouts in their striking scarlet dress uniforms and quaint Scottish style caps. The corps badge is an anchor superimposed by two crossed rifles over traditional crossed black Marine ribbons in memory of British Admiral Horatius Nelson. Their elite police company provides escort duty on sparkling vintage Harley Davidson motorcycles, and their martial and symphonic bands are included among the world's best.

The Fuzileiros are descendants of what are perhaps the first modern marine corps units in the western world, the ubiquitous Natural Infantry Tercios created by the Portuguese admiralty in 1618 to protect the fleet against buccaneers. First employed on land against the Dutch invaders in Bahia, the Portuguese Tercios were from the start closely linked to operations on the Brazilian coastline.

When Regent Prince John VI arrived in Rio de Janeiro in 1808, he was escorted by the faithful Royal Naval Brigade. The unit was swiftly put into action providing the bulk of forces engaged in battles for French forts on the northeastern South American coast. These actions eventually led to the fall of Cayenne and the creation of what is today the large Amazonian state of Amapá.

Upon returning from French Guyana in 1809, the Marine unit was permanently stationed at Ilha das Cobras, "Island of Snakes" in front of downtown Rio de Janeiro.

On D. Pedro's declaration of independence in 1822, Portugueseforces were held in check by units which included the Naval Fusiliers of the Royal Naval Brigade who chose to support the new emperor. In Bahia, where the bloodiest combat occurred, the marines bore most of the fight to dislodge Portuguese troops, and consolidate the entire Brazilian coastline.

The imminent struggle for the southern province of Cisplatina saw the marines in action against Argentine naval and land forces. Although the land campaign did not go well, naval operations, usually involving marines, were decided in favor of the powerful Brazilian fleet.

Under international mediation the sovereign state of Uruguay was created, but it would be a long time before it became peaceful. In coastal patrols for slaverunners trying to break the imperial blockade despite its strict abolitionist laws, Brazilian marines acquired constant combat readiness.

In 1851 Argentine dictator Juan Manuel Rosas, joined forces with the Uruguayan rebel leader Manuel Oribe. But the marines were once again ready, participating in a multiforce campaign in the southern Pampas of Uruguay and at the mouth of the River Plate. Together with the forces loyal to Uruguayan president Don Joaquim Suarez, Brazilian troops forced the river pass of Tonelero, finally pushing for a decisive victory at Monte Caseros and returning peace to the region.

In 1864 Uruguay once again became a battlefield. Uruguayan President Aguirre received a Brazilian ultimatum to stabilize his small nation. His reply was to return the document so that it "would not remain in the republic's archives."

The Brazilian fleet stationed at the mouth of the River Plate, moved to support the rebel Uruguayan leader Venâncio Flores. After several landings and small encounters its marine units approached the apparently impregnable fortress city of Paissandu. So powerful were the defensive positions that the soldiers soon named it Sebastopol, in honor of the Crimean city which had fallen after a horrifying campaign only ten years earlier.

Facing the Brazilian marines, were more than 1.200 heavily armed infantrymen holding the ramparts with the help of fifteen cannon. Flanks guarding approaches to the fort were patrolled by cavalry, while forward guerrilla skirmishers formed a picket line just outside the high walls. Seven hundred marines advanced alone before seven hundred Uruguayan rebels under Flores could join them.

The one to one ratio greatly favored the defenders. All available men joined the attacking force and the fleet was able to land another hundred marines and one hundred rifle armed sailors. Only absolutely essential personnel stayed behind to man the ship's artillery. Under scorching heat and through irregular terrain, Brazilian forces advanced on their objective. Fatigued by the arducus march, the troops had to fight for eight hours before finally dislodging the advance picket line in a last, desperate charge. By nightfall no more Uruguayan troops remained outside the ramparts.

At five the next morning another hundred marines arrived on the battlefield, a much needed reinforcement to the attacking force. At nine the fleet began a violent bombardment, forcing the defenders to take cover as the marines charged. The defenders fought back tenaciously, catching the attackers midway with a deadly fusillade. By three thirty that afternoon, the fighting turned into a violent stalemate.

At this point, Marine Sergeant Francisco Borges de Souza exploited a momentary breach in the defensive lines amd his platoon succeeded in lowering the Uruguayan flag. Motivated by this, the entire force swarmed in behind, taking the fort which commanded the highest ground above the city and opening the way to final victory.

Paissandu fought on bravely, but finally fell after another month of bloody combat. Although wounded in the final attack, Sergeant Borges lived to fight in the Paraguayan War several years later. Sergeant Borges' bravery is responsible for the Brazilian naval tradition, in which the lowering of the national flag is always performed by four sergeants of "irreproacheable conduct".

During the Paraguayan War against Lopez, the marines saw almost continuous action. They defended the fleet against raiders, and took part in savage river battles in the Paraguayan basin. Marine troops, along with enemy prisoners, also built the five mile (eight kilometer) Chaco railroad. This enabled supplies to be ferried to forces upriver from the fortress at Humaita, helping to keep up a relentless bombardment behind the Paraguayan rear.

Throughout Brazil's many years of political unrest, the marines never faltered in duties and helped to bring the country into a more prosperous future. At the beginning of World War II a small detachment was sent to the isolated Atlantic island of Trindade, to prevent it from becoming a German U-boat base. In 1965 peacekeeping duty in the Dominican Republic kept the marines constantly under fire. But eventually, they were able to at last enjoy a lasting period of peace in which the corps was fully modernized. Well trained and equipped, the Fuzileiros Navais are an elite among Brazil's armed forces.

"Do your duty come what may!" Lance in hand, the Dragoon Guard at Brasilia's Presidential Palace march toward the palace ramp. The Dragoons of the Brazilian army still wear the original Austrian influenced uniforms. The feather colors help identify rank and duty. Officers wear yellow feathers, the men bear red and the fanfarre carries green. The unit's commanding officer uses the sole white feathered helmet. Although the Dragoons are named after light French troops of the eighteenth century, the golden Dragon that adorns their helmets comes from the heraldic Dragon used by the Portuguese Royal house of Bragança. Dom Pedro the First was a member. French horns are part of the extremely popular Dragoon fanfarre which plays everything from military marches to sambas, and Brazilian country hits.

Once every six months, the guard at Brasilia's Presidential Palace rotates between the Dragoons and the Presidential Guard Battalion. The officer of the unit going off duty ceremonially hands over the palace ramp to the officer of the unit taking charge. The ramp is then guarded for the president's traditional arrival Mondays and departure on Fridays. The Presidential Guard Battalion, popularly known as the Grenadiers, evokes memories with their uniforms of the bloody Paraguayan War.

CHILE
The Unbeaten
General Bernardo O'Higgins Military School
The Chilean Army NCO School

The neatly ranked troops goose stepping in perfect synch to martial music in the background immediately recall old Third Reich newsreels. In Prussian gray with their archtypic "Fritz" helmets and gleaming Mauser rifles, the Chilean army maintains German traditions that elsewhere have faded after two World Wars. Some units even use the 1870 Prussian "Pickelhaube" spike topped helmet. The nation's military academy parades in elegant blue tunics, white trousers and helmets similar to the "Albert" worn by the British Household Cavalry - another German design. Chile's army is dazzling.

When the great Inca Empire of the Peruvian Highlands decided to probe southward, they met the fierce Araucanians of the Chilean central valley. No effort could dislodge these ferocious Chilean tribes and the Incas were forced to retreat to their own territory, decisively beaten.

In 15[illegible]3 the Spaniards defeated the Incas, taking their gold and silver. Lusting for more precious metal, they also marched southward to see what they could find, and Pedro de Valdivia founded what is present day Santiago. They also encountered the stubborn Araucanians, and six months later Santiago was a pile of smouldering ruins. The Spaniards did not give up however, and soon Valdivia was back with more men, ready not only to rebuild the destroyed city but to build further settlements along the central valley. Valdivia was soon killed by the proud indians he tried to subdue.

The Spaniards never did defeat the Araucanians and for the next three hundred years, southern Chile was a battleground. With Napoleon's invasion of the Iberian Penninsula, in the early 1800's, many of Spain's South American colonies saw the chance to revolt. Local landowners formed independent governments and effortlessly pushed out the Spaniards. Because of internal bickering, the young patriot army was soon smashed by Spanish troops dispatched from Peru at the Battle of Rancagua.

Bernardo O'Higgins and San Martin defeat the Spanish at Maipú, 1818.

A few years later, the Chilean leaders who had fled eastward across the Andes joined forces with Argentina's José de San Martin and the Army of the Andes, and recrossed the Andes against Spain's royalists. Led by Bernardo O'Higgins, the son of an Irish immigrant, the Chilean forces joined San Martin at the battles of Chacabuco and Maipú. They decisively defeated the Royalist armies in 1818.

Years of civil unrest followed but no foreign power threatened Chile. In 1836 opposing the Peru and Bolivia Confederation, the Chilean army went to war and, two years after initial setbacks, captured the Peruvian capital, Lima. The 8,000 strong confederation army soon recaptured the city and forced a standoff with 4,500 Chileans who, due to supply and sanitary problems, retreated to the Huaylas and Libertad departments. There they regrouped to await 2,000 reinforcements from the south.

On 6 January 1839 Bolivian General Santa Cruz sensed a chance of cutting the Chileans to pieces before the arrival of reinforcements. He attacked a forward unit of 1,400 men as they crossed the Buin River. Most of the ferocious fighting which followed took place at a strategic stone bridge defended by eleven men of the Carampangue Battalion under command of Lieutenant Colipi, the son of an important Araucanian Chieftain. Throughout the day, Lieutenant Colipi's small rearguard fought off wave after wave of Bolivian attackers while the bulk of the Chilean army marched away rather than do battle at this tactically unfavorable position.

When night fell, the last of the Chilean columns had passed through. With the Bolivians still at bay, Colipi's eleven men had time to blow up the bridge and make a hasty escape.

At the battle of Yungay on 20 February 1839, the Chileans under the brilliant General Bulnes finally smashed the confederation army. The troops of the Buin River had arrived intact at the Yungay battlefield where they helped to destroy General Santa Cruz's army once and for all. Told of his son's gallant action, the old Indian chief shrugged it off, "Of course, he's my son. What else did you expect!" The Chilean army maintains the stiff resolve of the Araucanians to this day.

A distaff story of Chilean heroism during the Confederation War is about Sergeant Candelaria Pérez. The immigrant owner of a Chilean cafe in the Lima suburb of Callao, she heard of General Bulnes' advancing troops and immediately began collecting military information on Peru's army. She was imprisoned by the Peruvians, and freed after the battle of Guias.

As a sergeant, she fought with the Carampangue regiment throughout the campaign. At Yungay, it was Sergeant Candelaria Perez commanding a handful of men who took the strategic Pan de Azúcar heights under intense fire.

Forty years later, disputes over the Atacama Desert deposits of nitrate and borax at Antofagasta, Tarapacá, Tacna, and Arica once more led Chile into war with Bolivia. Peru sided with Bolivia, honoring a secret mutual defense pact and the bloody five-year War of the Pacific got underway.

The first phase detonated when Peruvian and Bolivian forces took property belonging to Chilean nitrate companies. The opening moves took place at sea.

The result was the complete destruction of Peru's powerful fleet, giving Chile mastery of the Pacific Coast. The land phase began with Chilean troops steamrolling northward to take Antofagasta and Tarapacá. Chilean forces disembarked and took the cities of Tacna

The Corvo is the Chilean army's fighting knife.

and Arica on the southern Peruvian coast after storming the incredibly steep Alliança heights under ferocious fire from above. Their daring attack decisively defeated the Bolivians who lost control over their Pacific coast to Chile.

The Peruvians fought on, but another Chilean sea borne expedition of 25,000 landed at Pisco and gained victory at Chorillos and Lima.

Their capital lost, the army cut to pieces after the final battle at Miraflores, stragglers from Peru's army and indians from the mountains took to the Sierras to fight a war of attrition. The Chilean army decided not to follow them into the difficult and dangerous terrain, instead it set up advanced outposts between the mountains and the coastal plain to serve as a picket line and supply network to consolidate the captured territory.

One of these small garrison towns, La Concepcion, was manned by a seventy seven man contingent of Chilean soldiers from the Chacabuco regiment, mostly youngsters from sixteen to twenty one. Early on a warm July afternoon they were attacked by a veteran force of 3,000 Peruvian rebels and Indians. Following the initial skirmish, the Peruvians made offers to accept surrender which were duly refused.

For two days the small force resisted countless debilitating charges. With all their ammunition gone, five surviving Chileans unsheathed their swords and fought a human wave that eventually overwhelmed them. No prisoners were taken, not even an army nurse, of the famous **Cantineras**, who accompanied troops to the front. Sensing the arrival of a relief column, the Peruvians rapidly left the battlefield, leaving arriving reinforcements with a scene of complete destruction. Deeply touched by the heroism and tenacity of the teenaged defenders, the troops removed the young hearts of the fallen so that they could be buried in their native land. The troops pursued the elusive Peruvians with such a vengeance that all resistance quickly dissolved. To this day, Chile's army swears allegiance to the flag on the seventh of July, in honor of those seventy seven heroes who perished in the highlands of Peru. The war, although bloody and brutal, increased Chile's size by more than a third, and further cemented the Chilean army's myth of invincibility.

During the War of the Pacific the famous Chilean **Corvo** Combat Knife was used to great effect. An adaptation of tools of miners from the Pampas of Atacama who used whatever they could to fight off Bolivian and Peruvian raiders, it became the standard fighting knife of the Chilean army. Curved like a Condor's claw it soon evolved, into a knife with a thinner blade and grip. Chilean soldiers devised special fighting techniques with drills which would imbed the curved point into an enemy's chest with a hammering action. Engineers charged steep hills using the corvo like an ice climbing pick. They slashed the bottom sandbagged positions with their sturdy blades, collapsing the upper layers thus opening way for the assaulting troops close behind.

Today, the **Corvo** is a permanent piece of the Chilean soldier's uniform,and the precise, deadly drills have evolved into a unique form of martial arts. The Corvo has quasi mythical significance for the Chilean soldier much as the Dirk and the Kukri have for the Scots and Gurkhas.

There were no more external threats until the 1970's and 80's when border disputes with Argentina over the Southern Beagle Channel flared. Although the problem was peacefully negotiated in 1982, Chile saw much internal unrest until 1973 when a military junta led by General Augusto Pinochet Ugarte overthrew left wing president Salvador Allende. The country returned to stability until 1989 when the current president, Patricio Aylwin was elected by popular vote.

Foreign and domestic threats have shown Chile's army to be one of the most professionally led and trained in Latin America. Well defended by the massive Andes to the west, the scorching Atacama Desert to the north and the antarctic islands to the south, Chile is a long thin strip of land surrounded by encroaching neighbors. Unbeaten and currently enjoying good diplomatic relations with its neighbors, Chile's army is well versed in the subtleties of South American politics.

It boasts crack army units equipped with advanced French AMX -30 medium battle tanks and Brazilian EE-9 Cascavel and EE-11 Urutu armoured vehicles for the north. Superbly trained and equipped mountain specialists guard the Andean passes while

Chilean troops parade on National Day.

Detail of a cadet's uniform.

professional paratroop and special forces troops are ready for quick deployment. Chile's Army, conscious of its geographically difficult situation, intends to make sure that the tradition of invincibility continues.

The Santiago neighborhood of Las Condes is perhaps the most elegant in the wide avenued city. Its vast parks and clean promenades give onto vistas of the snow topped **Cordillera** on rare days when Santiago's thick wall of smog has been magically washed away by the rain. An imposing, mysterious grey building on Apoquindo Street commands the neighborhood.

Above pillars of cold grey concrete, is the name of the school for an unbeaten army: **Escuela Militar del Libertador General O'Higgins.**(General O'Higgins,the Liberator's Military School), Chile's counterpart to Sandhurst, West Point and St.Cyr. Since 1832 it has rapidly earned a name for educational quality throughout the Americas.

The cadets lined up for morning drill reflect a distant and very different past. In Prussian grey and 1870 style **Pickelhaube** spike helmets, the young Chilean soldiers resonate with Bismarck's rise to power. Although photographs of the War of the Pacific show the Chilean Army in blue and crimson uniforms of French origin typical throughout Latin America, the stunning Prussian victory in the 1870-1871 Franco Prussian War impressed the Chilean high command.

The arrival in 1886 of a Prussian Captain named Emil Koerner to reform the **Escuela Militar** changed Chilean Military tradition forever. Koerner rose rapidly in the ranks thanks mainly to his help in winning the 1891 civil war against the authoritarian president Balmaceda. Koerner became Chief of General Staff and installed Prussian training methods, uniforms a nd traditions enthusiastically received by the young Chilean officer corps.

A fine example of the morale of Chilean cadets comes from the **Alpatacal** defillade tragedy. One day in the early years of this century a detachment of young cadets from the Escuela Militar playfully relaxed on a train crossing the steep frozen Andes h alfway between Santiago and Mendoza in Argentina. They were on their way to a parade before their Argentine neighbors in commemoration of their joint struggle for Chile's independence. A sharp turn toppled the train. The body count began to grow, to the horror of the officers in command as the wreck was cleared. Despite the overwhelming number of dead cadets, the decision was made on the spot, to carry on with the mission. In mourning, many cadets in bandages and torn uniforms, the young Chileans paraded through the streets of Mendoza to the thunderous cheers of an emotional crowd.

In a central Santiago area, lies the **Escuela de Suboficiales** where non commissioned officers are formed. Uniforms here are 1930's German style,and the stiff legged German goose stepped form of marching is standard. Obvious German influences are the old Prussian Mauser rifles, kept in pristine condition, and the unique **Schwalbenest**, (Swallow's Nest) band members wear over the upper arm.

Members of the present German army who have viewed precision Chilean military drill have confessed deep emotion on seeing their age old traditions reborn. The elegance and marching skill of the Chilean army on parade, with a backdrop of snow white Andean peaks, is a stirring and memorable spectacle.

(Previous Spread) Officers and cadets at the Escuela de Suboficiales (Non Commissioned Officers School) proudly parade the flag on a cold Santiago morning. Young cadets at Chile's military school renew the spirit of their country's glorious military past. (Facing) On parade, the School's commander stands out clearly. He alone wears handpicked white ostrich feathers on his spiked helmet. (This Page Left) Clad in his elegant dark blue tunic, the Tambor Mayor, or Drum Major, of the Military School concentrates before leading the parade on Chile's National Day. The band uses red horse hair on their helmets, while the troops wear white. (Below) "Pickelhaube" helmet similar to the 1870 Prussian model. Nowhere in the world is German military tradition practiced to such perfection.

(Previous Spread) In a scene reminiscent of the long gone Nuremberg Rallies, Chilean soldiers assemble for a briefing. Note the white packs reminiscent of the War of the Pacific, and worn today only on ceremonial occasions. (Left) The Military School's Drum Major in his service uniform. Note the Schwalbenest stripes on his upper arm. (Above) The elegant Cabeza de Leon (Lion Head) sword of the Military School. (Bottom) Clad in Gala Blues, the cadets of the Military School approach the reviewing stand. (Facing) With the majestic Andes in the background, young cadets on parade.

(Top Left) An NCO School cadet, holds the "Arbol de Campanas" or Tree of Bells, an ancient musical instrument of the Roman Legions, used for marching in cadence. (Top Right) Bugler's Colors. Underneath the Chilean Army badge lies the nation's motto, "Por la Razon o la Fuerza"- (Through Right or through Force). (Below left) High ranking officers parade in gala white. (Bottom Right) German style bayonet. (Facing) Other than the Chilean army badge on the helmet, this young NCO could easily be mistaken for a member of the Wehrmacht.

Acknowledgements

Lt. Col. Mariano Bronenberg
(Argentine Army)

Col. Alberto Luis Devoto
(Argentine Army)

Col. Newton Bonumá dos Santos
(Brazilian Army)

Col. Gastão Puchalski Lopes
(Brazilian Army)

Com. Jaime Martins da Motta Neto
(Brazilian Marine Corps)

Cap. Paulo Roberto Marcos Quintão
(Brazilian Marine Corps)

Cst. Steve Brown
(R.C.M.P.)

Brig. Pedro Collado Marti
(Chilean Army)

Lt. Col. Gabriel Vergara Cifuentes
(Chilean Army)

Maj. Jesper Gram Andersen
(Danish Army)

Lt. Col. Michel Muraton
(French Army)

Cp. Jacques Lorho
(French Foreign Legion)

Asp. Digeon
(French Army)

Col. J. W. S. Trelawny
(British Army)

Maj. Mike Gouldstone
(British Army)

Cap. (QGO) Sarankumar Limbu
(7 Gurkha Rifles - British Army)

Yeoman Quartermaster H. A. Thompson (British Army)

James J. Aktsoglou (Greek Army)

Col. Aditya Singh (Indian Army)

Cap. Rathore (Indian Army)

Gen. Gualtiero Stefanon (Italian Army)

Col. Mini (Italian Army)

Maj. Mamoru Fujisaki (Japan Self Defense Force)

Col. Ben Kharaba Abdelkader (Moroccan Army)

Com. José Luis Gamboa Ballester (Spanish Navy)

Maj. Christian Braunstein and Skrallan (Swedish Army)

Cap. Mike Everett (United States Army)

Lt. Jim Dolan (United States Army)

M. Sgt. William Stanley Smith Jr. (United States Army)

SSGT. Hal Freeman (U.S.M.C.)

Cpl. Joey Benford (U.S.M.C.)